Cookbook For Teens

Teens Cook Easy Cooking
for Young Adults
Ultimate Teen Recipes Cookbook

Julia Moore

Copyright Legal Information

Table of Contents

Introduction

SIMPLE AND DELICIOUS

Welcome to the Cookbook for Teens. The recipes in this cookbook is curated and designed for easy everyday cooking.

The world's top chefs had to start somewhere, therefore this will be the perfect first cookbook an introduction to the art of cooking, you will learn introductory preparation and cooking techniques, and learn about seasoning and measuring recipes, and much, much, more!

In this recipe book you will find delicious meals that could easily be prepared and cooked in your kitchen, hassle free. With this little cookbook you will be inspired to love your kitchen and bond with your family.

In here, you will find recipes for your favorite meat and seafood dishes, curries, chilies and pastas! If you are feeling more adventurous and need a quick pick-me-up then the Butter Chicken recipe or the Jumbo Shrimp Curry might be just what you need for an after school pick-me-up. No matter how you are feeling, there is a recipe to suit your every mood and taste bud!

The recipe collection are also very versatile and would make great lunches, weekend dinners and even holiday feasts that will surely impress your relatives and friends!

We sincerely hope you enjoy this Cookbook for Teens as much as we did cooking our way through all these great recipes.

Disclaimer: Cook times and Prep times are suggested times based on trial and preferences that have been adjusted by our team. We have provided "Notes" sections in the recipes for you to add in your own personal tips and tricks on how to make *your* perfect dinner entrée.

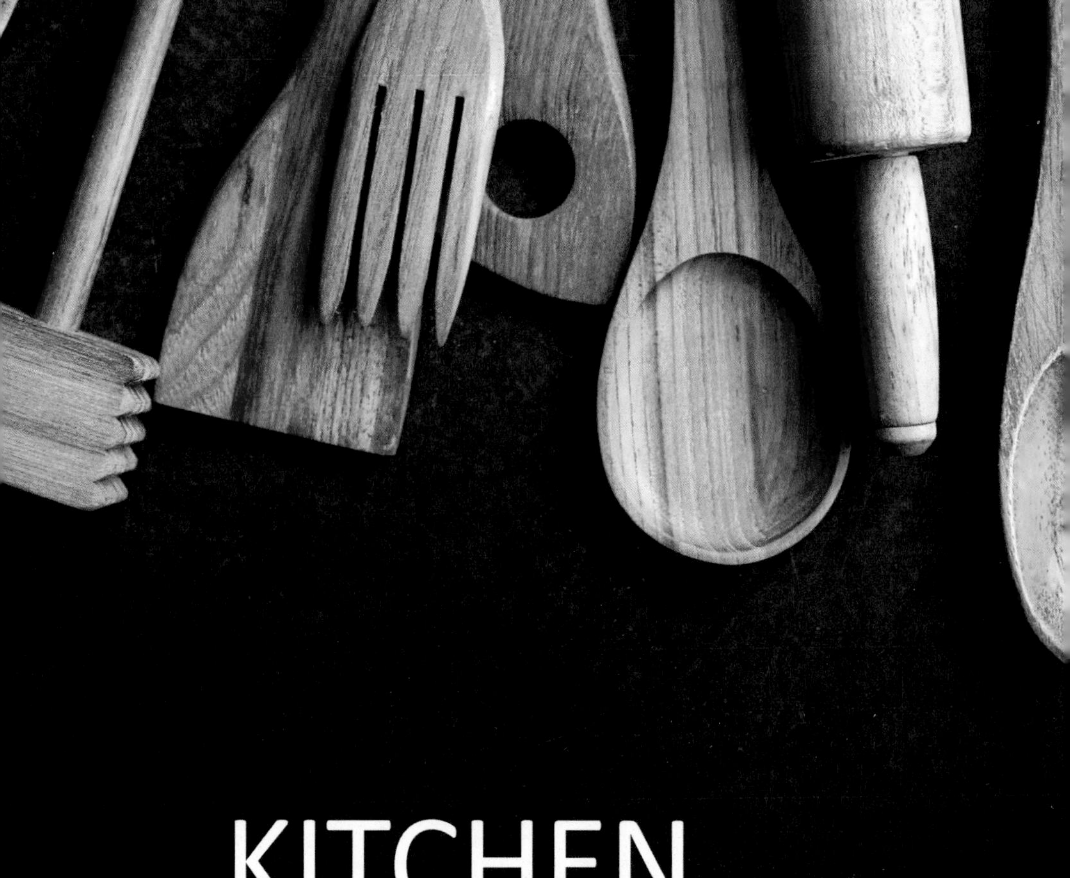

KITCHEN ESSENTIALS

Pasta Measurements

The Pasta Measurements are for 2 servings

LONG PASTAS	DRY PASTA Measured with Hand	COOKED PASTA Measured in Cups
Angel Hair	2 to 3inches (circumference)	2 cups
Fettuccine	2 to 3inches (circumference)	2 cups
Linguine	2 to 3inches (circumference)	2 cups
Spaghetti	2 to 3inches (circumference)	2 cups
Thin Spaghetti	2 to 3inches (circumference)	2 cups

The Pasta Measurements are for 2 servings

SHORT PASTAS	DRY PASTA Measured in Cups
Macaroni Elbows	2 cups
Penne	2 cups
Rigatoni	2 cups
Rotini	2 cups
Farfalle	2 cups
Fusilli	2 cups

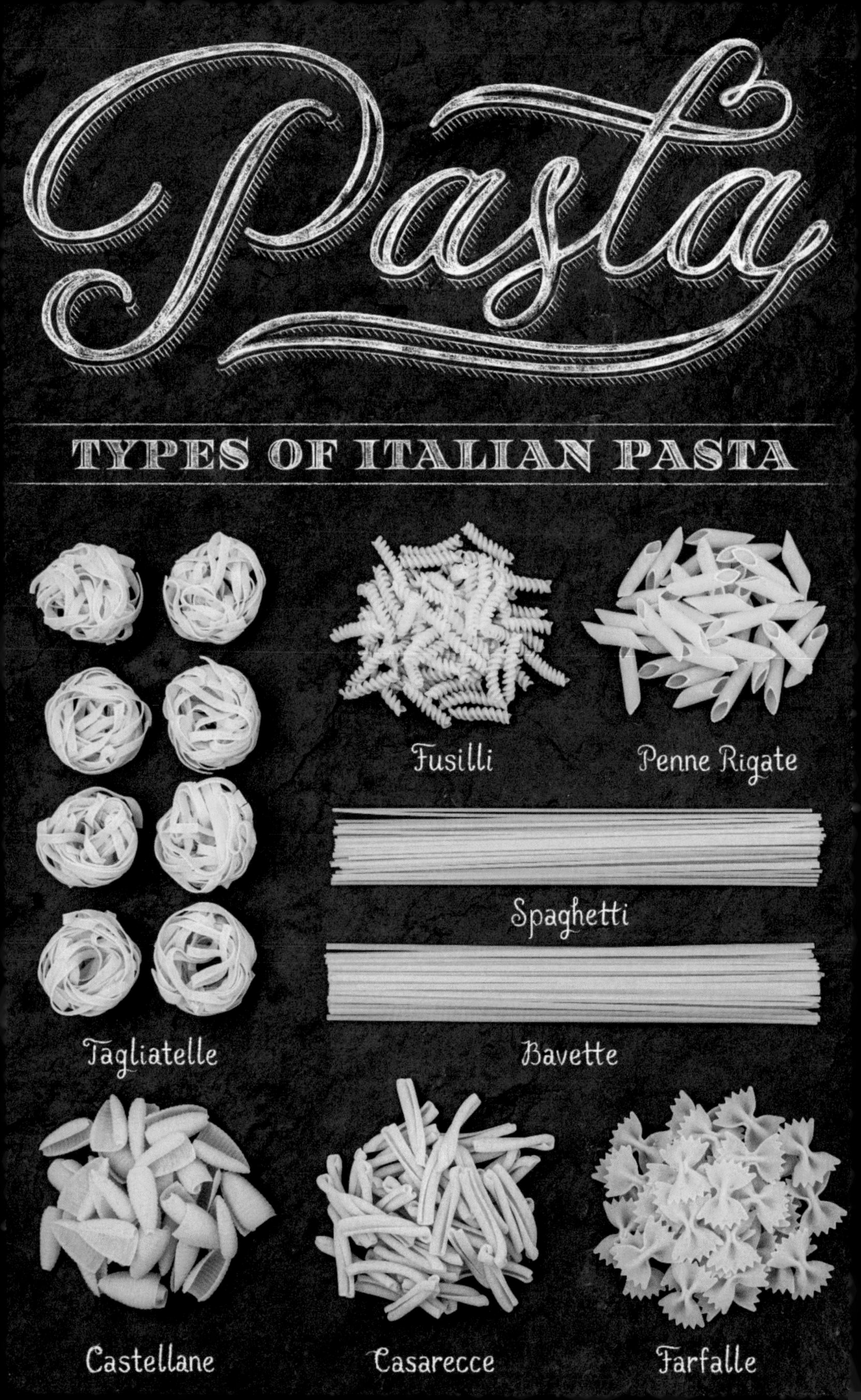

TYPES OF ITALIAN PASTA

Fusilli

Penne Rigate

Spaghetti

Tagliatelle

Bavette

Castellane

Casarecce

Farfalle

Cooking Terminology

Al dente
Food cooked until it is firm to the bite. Commonly used to describe how pasta should be cooked.

Baste
Spoon juices over food that is being roasted or baked to prevent from drying out. Commonly used when baking meats.

Blanch
Plunge food into boiling water briefly, and then removed and placed into cold water to stop the cooking process.

Deglaze
To add wine, stock or other liquid to the cooking juices left in a pan after roasting or sautéing, it's heated again to make a jus.

Fold
A gentle hand mixing method used to combine a lighter, airy mixture (e.g. whipped eggs or whipped cream) with a heavier mixture. The motion is top to bottom (as if 'folding' a towel) rather than round and round.

Glaze
To coat foods with a syrup, before or after cooking.

Infuse
To extract flavor from one food into another, often by heating or steeping.

Julienne
To cut vegetables into long thin matchsticks.

Marinate
Leave food soaked in a sauce/liquid and other flavorings to give it more flavor.

Panfry
Cook quickly in heated pan (usually on High heat) using a small amount of oil or butter.

Poach
To cook very gently in simmering water or other liquid e.g.: wine.

Purée
To blend well cooked fruits or vegetables into a thick smooth paste.

Reduce
To boil rapidly in order to evaporate liquid, and thicken the sauce.

Roux
A method of thickening a sauce by combining flour or cornstarch with water and gradually stirring it into the sauce.

Sauté
To quickly fry food in a hot pan.

Sear
To brown meats in a hot pan or on a grill.

Simmer
To cook in a hot liquid that is heated to the point where little bubbles rise to the surface.

Steam
To cook in the steam created by boiling water in a large pot/pan.

Steep
To immerse food in hot liquid to extract the flavour.

Stir-fry
Traditionally cooked in a wok, where small pieces of food are cooked at a high turning and tossing constantly until cooked.

Whip
To beat with an egg-beater or electric beater until thick and frothy.

Whisk
To beat with a wire whisk until thick or frothy.

Zest
The outer rind of citrus fruit containing essential oils. Mostly used for garnish or in baking.

Your Own Cooking Terminology	

Conversion and Ingredients Measurements

Canned Soups and Sauces used in this cookbook
The sizes used in this recipe is 14 oz. (Equivalent to 1 and ¾ cups)

Frozen Bagged Vegetables used in this cookbook
The sizes used is 14 oz. this typically feeds about 4 people (or 2 really hungry teenagers)

Optimum Servings for the recipes used in this cookbook
The ideal portion size in this recipe cookbook is between 4 to 8 servings. The reason behind this is to not over crowd your food when cooking.

CONVERSION TABLE

LENGTH		
INCHES	DECIMAL	MM
1/16	0,06	1,59
1/8	0,13	3,18
3/16	0,19	4,76
1/4	0,25	6,35
5/16	0,31	7,94
3/8	0,38	9,53
7/16	0,44	11,11
1/2	0,50	12,70
9/16	0,56	14,29
5/8	0,63	15,88
11/16	0,69	17,46
3/4	0,75	19,05
13/16	0,81	20,64
7/8	0,88	22,23
15/16	0,94	23,81
1	1,00	25,40

WEIGHT	
IMPERIAL	METRIC
1/2 oz	15 g
1 oz	29 g
2 oz	57 g
3 oz	85 g
4 oz	113 g
5 oz	141 g
6 oz	170 g
8 oz	227 g
10 oz	283 g
12 oz	340 g
13 oz	369 g
14 oz	397 g
15 oz	425 g
1 lb	453 g
1 1/2 lb	680 g
2,2 lb	1 kg

TEMPERATURE	
FAHRENHEIT	CELSIUS
5	-15
10	-12
25	-4
50	10
100	37
150	65
200	93
250	121
300	150
325	160
350	180
375	190
400	200
425	220
450	230
500	260

Know Your Knives

Bread Knife

Carving Knife

Cleaver

Santoku Knife

Chef Knife

Boning Knife

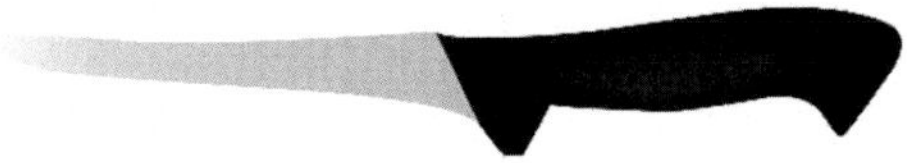

Utility Knife

Filleting Knife

Small Pairing Knife

Coriander
Dried coriander seeds are a staple in South East Asian cooking and is found in garam masala and other Indian curries. The fresh coriander leaves are used mostly as a garnish or added to broths to give it a more citrus note.

Cayenne Pepper
Common spice found in hot sauces and is usually sprinkled onto sandwiches or pastas to add a spicy flavor.

Sage
Savory and peppery, it is also a staple in Italian cooking and goes great with meat and fish dishes as well as on grilled vegetables.

Curcuma/Turmeric
Also known as turmeric and is found in a lot of South East Asian cuisines such as Thai curries and dishes.

Star Anise
Used both in culinary and medicinal cooking and is a very popular Asian spice especially in Vietnamese noodle soups.

What's in Your Spice Rack?

Ginger
Whether it's fresh or ground into a powder, ginger is an essential spice for cooking seafood (it helps minimize the 'fishy-ness' of the seafood) and is a staple in a lot of curries and Asian cooking.

Cinnamon
Mostly used in baking and in coffees and teas, it's a wonderful spice to add aroma to your stews and desserts.

Chili
Fresh and dried chilies are used in a variety of dishes, and adds a spicy kick to meats, vegetables and even desserts.

Oregano
Oregano is a common herb in Italian cuisines and go great in pizza sauce and grilled vegetables, meat and fish.

Saffron
Saffron has a delicious honey and grassy notes to it and is a beloved spice of Asian and Middle Eastern cuisines. It's commonly used in baking and flavoring rice and pastas.

What's in Your Spice Rack?

Bay Leaf
This aromatic spice goes great in meat sauces, and thick pasta sauces. It's also a favorite in hearty stews and stocks.

Dried/Fresh Garlic
Aromatic and delicious in just about anything. Dried garlic is very easy to use to season and marinate meats, fish and vegetables.

Paprika
Favorite spice used to season rice, stews and sausages.

Black Pepper
Popular spice used to season foods and is a staple in every kitchen.

Pink Salt
Commonly used as a brine and has more health benefits compared to table salt.

Basil
Fresh basil is used in pastas, pizzas and stews. It is also a main ingredient in pesto.

Sea Salt
Used in roasting and as a brine for a variety of meats and seafood.

Cumin
Mainly used for highly spiced foods and is a popular spice in Indian, and Mexican cooking. It goes great with stews and grilled meats, especially lamb and chicken dishes.

Clove
Used in Asian and Middle Eastern cuisines in curries and marinades.

Nutmeg
A fragrant spice used mostly in baking and desserts, also a favorite in eggnog and other European cuisines.

Pressure Cooker Bone Broth Stocks

Follow this recipe to create your own healthy Bone Broths. This is an easy to follow Bone Broth recipe that you can make at home and use it as an alternative to store bought chicken, beef, or pork Bone Broths Homemade stocks.

INGREDIENTS

- 2 pounds fresh animal bones (either chicken, beef, pork etc.) You can inquire about fresh bones from your local butcher
- 2 purple onion, peeled and cut in half
- 2 large carrots, chopped into chunks
- 2 celery sticks cut in half
- ½ tablespoon sea salt

10 cups water

PREPARATION

1. For a clearer broth you will need to blanch the bones first. In a large soup pot, fill it halfway full and let it come to a boil. Once boiling add your bones into the pot and let it cook for about 5 minutes. Then strain and rinse the bones under cold running water for 5 minutes. This will wash away all the impurities of the animal bones.

2. Once done blanching add the bones to a cheesecloth along with your vegetable ingredients. Secure the bone broth bag with twine.

3. Add the water to your pressure cooking pot. Then add in your bone broth bag, sprinkle the sea salt and lock lid. Set to Soup and change the time to 90 minutes. Set timer. Once timer goes off, release pressure naturally. Let broth cool then remove the bone broth bag and bottle up your homemade bone broth in mason jars and keep refrigerated until use. Or you can freeze 2 cup portions of it in freezer containers.

Butter			
1 Stick	4 ounces	8 tablespoons	½ cup

Lemon		
1 Lemon	1 to 3 tablespoons juice	1 to 1 ½ teaspoons grated zest
4 Large Lemons	1 cup juice	¼ cup grated zest

Creams		
Half and Half	½ milk ½ cream	11-18% butter fat
Light cream		18% butter fat
Heavy Cream	Whipping cream	36% or more butter fat
Double Cream	Clotted or Devonshire	42% butter fat

Notes

BREAKFAST ESSENTIALS

Mornings are tough, but Breakfast shouldn’t be

Honey Toast with Berry Compote

COOK TIME
16 MIN
PREP TIME
10 MIN
SERVINGS
3-4 SERVINGS

INGREDIENTS

- 6 slices of thick multi-grain brown bread (choose your favorite)
- Soft butter for spreading
- 4 cups frozen mixed berries
- ½ cup brown sugar
- ½ teaspoon cinnamon
- 1 cup honey

PREPARATION

1. Preheat oven to 350 F (if you want to make smaller batches, you can use your toaster oven instead)

2. Butter all 6 of your sliced bread and lay them on a baking sheet and then even divide up the honey between the 6 slices. Drizzle the honey with a spoon. Sprinkle the cinnamon over your slices, and once your oven is preheated, place your slices in the middle rack and bake for 8 minutes. Set timer.

3. In a small sauce pan, bring to a boil about ½ cup of water to boil, then stir in your frozen mixed berries and brown sugar. And cook on medium heat, keep stirring for about 8 minutes, until you've reduced some of the liquid. Turn off heat and set it aside.

4. Once your timer goes off, your honey toast should be golden brown, take it out of the oven and plate 2 toast on each plate then spoon your berry compote over the toast. You can serve with yogurt and orange juice.

Open-Face Spinach and Feta Cheese Omelette

COOK TIME
10 MIN
PREP TIME
8 MIN
SERVINGS
2 SERVINGS

INGREDIENTS

- 6 large eggs
- 2 cups packed baby spinach
- 1 cup feta cheese, crumbled
- Butter for buttering the frying pan
- Salt and pepper to taste
- You will need a small 10 inch non-stick frying pan with a lid (or you can use a non-stick single serve frying pan, those come in 6-10 inch sizes)

PREPARATION

1. Crack 3 eggs each into 2 separate bowls and whisk until yolk and white is incorporated, about 1 minute. Set aside.

2. Heat up your non-stick frying pan and lightly butter the pan. Once butter is sizzling turn heat to low and pour the first bowl of eggs into the pan, then sprinkle about 1 cup of baby spinach over your eggs. Use a silicone spatula to lightly press the spinach down. Do not stir.

3. Cover the pan with the lid and let it cook on medium heat for about 4 minutes. Then lift up lid and add in about ½ cup of the crumbled feta and let it cook uncovered for another 4 to 5 minutes, until the feta becomes soft and your egg mixture becomes solid. Take it off the heat and using your silicone spatula, scrape the sides of your pan, and your open-face omelette should easily slide onto your serving plate (this is if you used a non-stick frying pan)

4. Repeat these steps to make the second batch of eggs.

5. Serve with fresh cracked pepper and sea salt along with toast and juice.

Delicious Oven Baked Eggs Many Ways

COOK TIME
10-15 MIN
PREP TIME
10 MIN
SERVINGS
2 SERVINGS

Baked Eggs Ingredient Combinations

2 eggs	**¼ cup sliced white mushrooms**	**¼ cup shaved cheddar**	**Couple drops of truffle oil**
2 eggs	**5 baby cherry tomatoes sliced in half**	**4 fresh basil leaves cut into strips**	**Crack of fresh pepper and sea salt**
2 eggs	**½ cup tomato sauce**	**¼ cup baby spinach roughly shopped**	**Crack of fresh pepper and sea salt**
2 eggs	**¼ cup baby shrimp**	**A few fresh chives, finely chopped**	**Drizzle sesame oil and fresh cracked pepper and sea salt**
2 eggs	**Couple slices of smoked salmon, roughly chopped**	**1 tablespoon capers**	**Crack of fresh pepper and sea salt**
2 eggs	**Couple slices of black forest ham, thinly sliced**	**½ cup arugula roughly chopped**	**Crack of fresh pepper and sea salt**

PREPARATION

1. Preheat your oven to 350 F and lightly oil 2 oven-proof ramekins. Add your choice of fillings into each ramekin then crack 2 eggs into it, with the seasonings.
2. Place in middle rack of hot oven and bake for about 10 minutes or until whites are set and the yolks is still runny. Serve with juice and toast.

French Toast with Cinnamon Apple Filling

COOK TIME
15 MIN
PREP TIME
10 MIN
SERVINGS
4-6 SERVINGS

INGREDIENTS

- 8 slices of white bread (choose your favorite) buttered lightly on both sides
- 4 eggs whisked with 1 tablespoon honey and 1 tablespoon of milk
- 2 green apples, peeled and sliced
- 1 cup water
- ¼ cup brown sugar
- 1 teaspoon cinnamon
- 1 tablespoon butter
- 2 cups heavy whipping cream
- You will need 2 baking sheets of the same size and an electric whisk to whisk the whipping cream
- 1 teaspoon vanilla extract

PREPARATION

1. Preheat oven to 350 F. Lightly oil your 2 baking sheets. Pour your whisked egg mixture into a shallow dish and dip both sides of your bread into the mixture – do this lightly – do not soak the bread. Lay the dipped bread onto your 2 baking sheets and in middle of rack side by side in your hot oven. Let it bake for 10 minutes set timer.

2. While your toast is baking. In a small sauce pan bring to a boil one cup of water and add in the butter, apples, brown sugar and cinnamon. Let it cook on medium heat for 10 minutes, or until the apples are soft. Take it off the heat and set aside.
3. In a large mixing bowl add your cream and vanilla extract and whisk until it forms stiff peaks. Keep refrigerated until ready to serve.

4. Check your toast to make sure they are golden brown. Remove from oven and place the first 4 slices on individual serving plates. Then evenly distribute your apple filling onto the 4 slices, then sandwich together with the second slice. Drizzle honey over your French toast and a pinch of cinnamon. Serve immediately with fresh whipped cream.

Tuna Fish Toast with Ricotta Cheese

COOK TIME
8-10 MIN
PREP TIME
5-8 MIN
SERVINGS
4 SERVINGS

INGREDIENTS

- 4 slices of sourdough (you can use practically any type of bread, but sourdough adds another depth of flavor)
- 2 cans chunk tuna, drained
- ½ cup light mayo
- 1 celery stick, finely chopped
- 1 pickle, finely chopped
- ¼ teaspoon salt
- ½ teaspoon pepper
- 1 teaspoon Dijon mustard
- 1 cup Ricotta cheese, drained

PREPARATION

1. Preheat oven to 350 F. Lightly butter your sourdough slices and place them on a baking sheet. Set aside.

2. In a large mixing bowl mix together the tuna, with mayo, then the celery, pickles, Dijon and Ricotta cheese. Once mixed, taste for seasoning, then add the salt and pepper accordingly.

3. Evenly spoon the tuna mixture on your sourdough slices, then bake in center rack in hot oven for 8 to 10 minutes. Set timer. Once timer goes off. Take it out and serve with fresh fruits and juice.

Notes

Healthy Breakfast On-The-Go Smoothies

COOK TIME
2-5 MIN
PREP TIME
5 MIN
SERVINGS
2-4 SERVINGS

Breakfast Fruit Smoothie Combinations

Very Berry Monster	**1 cup raspberries 1 cup blueberries 1 cup strawberries 1 cup blackberries**	**1 banana ½ cup sliced almonds**	**½ tablespoon honey and 1 cup plain Greek yogurt**
Mango Mama	**4 cups frozen mango, 1 cup apple juice**	**1 banana ½ cup coconut flakes**	**½ tablespoon honey and 1 cup milk**
Green Monster	**2 cups kiwi 2 cups green grapes 1 cup spinach**	**1 banana ¼ cup chia seeds**	**½ tablespoon honey 1 cup apple juice**
Peaches Madness	**4 cups peaches 1 cup pineapples**	**1 banana ½ cup sliced almonds**	**2 cups plain Greek yogurt**
Orange Bliss	**4 oranges, peeled and cut 1 cup pineapples**	**1 banana ½ cup baby carrots**	**1 cup orange juice and 1 cup plain Greek yogurt**
Strawberries and Cream	**4 cups frozen strawberries**	**1 banana 1 whole avocado, pitted, sliced**	**½ tablespoon honey and 1 cup strawberry Greek Yogurt**

PREPARATION

Choose your smoothie combination and put all the ingredients into a blender, and blend until smooth. It for breakfast or a quick snack after school. Enjoy!

GOURMET SANDWICHES

Anywhere – Anytime – Breakfast – Lunch – Dinner

Sourdough Prosciutto Grilled Cheese

COOK TIME
5-8 MIN
PREP TIME
10 MIN
SERVINGS
2 SERVINGS

INGREDIENTS

- 4 slices of sourdough (you can use practically any type of bread, but sourdough adds another depth of flavor to the overall sandwich)
- This recipe is designed to make 2 sandwiches (either for lunch or dinner). Adjust the ingredients accordingly for more servings.
- 4 slices of sharp Monterey Jack cheese (choose your favorite)
- 4 slices of Prosciutto
- Small handful of arugula
- Soft Butter for spreading
  Fresh cracked pepper to taste

PREPARATION

1. Butter both sides of the sourdough bread generously, and set them aside. Heat a non-stick frying pan on medium. Once it's hot drizzle a very small amount of olive oil and use a thick piece of paper towel to spread the oil around the pan. You just need to lightly grease it.

2. Then place either 2 or 4 slices onto your frying pan (if your pan isn't big enough then only place 2 slices). Gently brown each side of the sourdough and add a crack of fresh pepper onto one side of the sourdough, reduce your heat by half. (1-2 minutes each side or until golden brown)

3. **Begin layering the ingredients onto your sourdough while still in the frying pan in this order:**

- Monterey Jack Cheese
- Arugula
- 2 slices of Prosciutto
- Monterey Jack Cheese

4. Once you are done layering onto the first slice of sourdough, cover it with the second slice and gently press down on it. Grill each side again for about 1 minute, or until the Monterey Jack Cheese has melted. Repeat the process for your second sandwich. Serve with a side of pickles or garden salad.

Smoked Salmon and Spinach Grilled Cheese

COOK TIME
10 MIN
PREP TIME
10 MIN
SERVINGS
6 SERVINGS

INGREDIENTS

- This recipe is designed to make 6 sandwiches (either for lunch or dinner). Adjust the ingredients accordingly to however many sandwiches you would like to serve or the number of people you intend to feed.
- 12 slices of multi-grain bread bruschetta (choose your favorite bread)
- 24 slices of sharp Monterey Jack cheese (choose your favorite)
- 1 package of sliced smoked salmon roughly 12 oz.
- ½ cup capers
- ½ cup thinly sliced onion (sliced into long strips)
- 1-2 cups packed baby spinach leaves
- Olive oil
- Fresh cracked pepper to taste

PREPARATION

1. Preheat your oven to 350 F. You will need 2 baking sheets of the same size. On the first baking sheet cover it with a layer of parchment paper and evenly lay out 6 of the bruschetta. Lightly drizzle olive oil over the bruschetta and give it a round of fresh cracked pepper.

2. **Begin layering the ingredients in this order:**

- Monterey Jack Cheese
- Baby spinach leaves
- 2-3 slices smoked salmon
- Sprinkle of capers and onions
- Monterey Jack Cheese

3. Repeat until you've layered all the bruschetta. Once layering is complete cover the layers with the second slice of the bruschetta and lightly drizzle olive oil over the tops of the bruschetta. Take your second baking sheet and lightly grease the bottom flat side of it with a paper towel and some olive oil. Then lightly press it over your bruschetta sandwiches, basically covering it.

4. Place the bruschetta sandwiched between the 2 baking sheets into the over and let it bake for 8-10 minutes or until cheese is melted.

5. Set timer. Once timer goes off, use oven mitts and carefully remove the baking sheets from the coven.

6. Remove the baking sheet covering the bruschetta (this helps keep the sandwich and ingredients in place and helps the cheese fuse with the bruschetta) Serve immediately with your favorite tomato soup!

This recipe is super versatile and you can substitute just about any of the ingredients.

Grilled Cheese Sandwich Combinations (2 Servings)

PROTIEN	VEGGIE	CHEESE	SEASONING
4 Slices of Black Forest Ham	4 Slices of Tomato	4 Slices of Sharp Cheddar	Fresh Cracked Pepper Soft Butter for Spreading Dijon for Spreading
4 Slices of Prosciutto	1 Cup Sun Dried Tomatoes, Drained	4 Slices of Swiss	Fresh Cracked Pepper Soft Butter for Spreading
4 Slices of Salami	1 Cup Sliced Cucumber, Divided	4 Slices of Pepper Jack	Fresh Cracked Pepper Soft Butter for Spreading
4 Slices of Turkey	1 Avocado, Sliced	4 Slices of Swiss	Half Apple Butter Half Soft Butter
4 Slices of Roast Beef	½ Cup Sun Dried Tomatoes mixed with ½ Cup Packed Arugula	4 Slices of Pepper Jack	Fresh Cracked Pepper Soft Butter for Spreading Dijon for Spreading
1 Cup Frozen baby shrimp, Thawed and Drained	1 Avocado, pitted and sliced	4 Slices of Provolone	Fresh Cracked Pepper Soft Butter for Spreading, Sprinkle Sea salt

Warm Chicken Salad Sandwiches

COOK TIME
15 MIN
PREP TIME
15 MIN
SERVINGS
4 SERVINGS

INGREDIENTS

- 2 medium sized chicken breasts, cut into strips
- 4 seeded bagels sliced in half (choose your favorite)
- 4 cups mixed arugula and baby spinach (or mixed greens, choose your favorite)
- 1 cup corn tidbits
- 2 avocados, cut and pitted
- 1 tablespoon lemon juice
- 1 teaspoon sesame oil
- 1 teaspoon soy sauce
- 1 teaspoon white pepper

The Dressing

- ½ cup sour cream
- 1 teaspoon dried parsley flakes
- 1 teaspoon oregano
- 1 teaspoon salt
- 1 teaspoon pepper

PREPARATION

1. In a mixing bowl quickly marinate your chicken strips with sesame oil, soy sauce and white pepper. Set aside.

2. In a smaller bowl, mashup the 2 avocados with a bit of lemon juice, keep refrigerated until ready to serve. Cook on high for 8 minutes. In another bowl whisk together the dressing ingredients and keep refrigerated until ready to serve.

3. Use a non-stick skillet and let it heat up over medium heat, once it's hot add a small drizzle of olive oil. Swirl it around your pan, then sauté your chicken strips. Flip them over with tongs and sauté for 10 minutes or until the meat has turned completely white. Once your chicken is cooked remove from heat into a large salad bowl. Let it cool for couple of minutes.

4. While your chicken is cooling, spread the mashed up avocado over your bagel halves. Once you're done spreading, add the corn and greens to your chicken along with the dressing and toss to mix. Then evenly distribute the chicken salad over your bagel along with couple cracks of fresh pepper. Sandwich everything together, cut in half and serve with a side of hot soup.

Amazing Sloppy Joes

COOK TIME
25 MIN
PREP TIME
15 MIN
SERVINGS
4-6 SERVINGS

INGREDIENTS

- 2 pounds ground beef
- Choose your favorite burger buns
- 1 cup ketchup
- 1 cup tomato paste
- 1 cup beef stock
- 1 large tomatoes, diced
- ½ cup diced red peppers and onions
- 1 teaspoon minced garlic
- 1 teaspoon oregano
- ½ tablespoon Worcestershire
- ½ tablespoon chili powder
- ½ teaspoon sriracha
- ½tablespoon yellow mustard

PREPARATION

1. Preheat your oven 350 F. Butter your burger buns, place them onto a baking sheet and bake in middle rack for about 8 minutes or until toasty.

2. In a mixing bowl whisk together your sauce ingredients in this order and set aside:

- Ketchup
- Tomato paste
- Worcestershire sauce
- Sriracha
- Yellow mustard
- Oregano
- Chili powder

3. In a large non-stick sauce pan heat up about ½ tablespoon of olive oil and sauté the ground beef for about 2 minutes on medium heat. Then add in your diced tomatoes, red peppers and onions and minced garlic and sauté for about 10 minutes to reduce the liquid. Slowly stir in your sauce into the meat mixture and turn the heat on high and keep stirring for another 10 minutes, until you have reduced most of the liquid. You want a thick meat sauce.

4. Your meat sauce should be finished in 20 to 25 minutes. Spoon the meat sauce onto your buns, and serve with a side salad or celery sticks.

Shrimp and Lobster Rolls

COOK TIME
8-10 MIN
PREP TIME
10 MIN
SERVINGS
4 SERVINGS

INGREDIENTS

- ½ pound baby shrimp, rinsed and drained
- ½ pound lobster meat (you can use frozen lobster meat or fresh from your local seafood grocer)
- 1 cup celery, finely diced
- ¼ cup fresh chives, finely chopped
- 1 tablespoon mayo
- 1 tablespoon lemon juice
- 1 teaspoon salt
- 1 teaspoon pepper
- Butter for spreading
- 4 long dinner rolls or hot dog buns (choose your favorite bread)

PREPARATION

1. Preheat oven 350 F and butter your dinner rolls. Place them on a baking sheet and bake in middle rack in your hot oven for about 8 minutes or until toasty warm. Once it's done turn off oven and leave the rolls in the oven to keep warm until ready to serve.
2. In a large mixing bowl, mix together the shrimp, lobster, celery, chives, mayo, lemon juice, salt and pepper. Once well mixed, evenly distribute your shrimp and lobster mixture in your dinner rolls. Serve immediately with extra lemon wedges.

Notes

EAT YOUR GREENS

Tasty Vegetable Appetizers, Lunches and Dinners

Green Apple and Smoked Salmon Salad

COOK TIME
IT'S A COLD SALAD
PREP TIME
10 MIN
SERVINGS
2 SERVINGS

INGREDIENTS

- 2 green apples, cored and sliced (no need to peel the apples)
- ¼ cup capers (optional)
- 1 head of romaine lettuce
- 500 grams smoked salmon

The Dressing

- 3 tablespoons olive oil
- 2 tablespoons fresh lemon juice
- 1 teaspoon lemon zest
- 2 tablespoon chopped fresh dill
- 1 teaspoon white pepper
- 1 teaspoon salt

PREPARATION

1. Cut off the stem of the romaine lettuce, then cut the bunch in half. Wash and rinse under cold water. Shake dry. Then chop up the romaine lettuce and place it in a salad bowl along with the sliced green apples.
2. In a smaller mixing bowl whisk together the dressing ingredients. Add it to your salad and toss evenly.
3. To serve: place the salad onto serve plates and add a few slices of smoked salmon and a sprinkle of capers and then a couple fresh cracked pepper and extra lemon wedges on the side.

Asian Sesame Cucumber Salad

COOK TIME
IT'S A COLD SALAD
PREP TIME
10 MIN
SERVINGS
4-6 SERVINGS

INGREDIENTS

- 4 long cucumbers, roughly the same size, washed
- 1 stalk green scallion, finely chopped
- About 1 cup chopped cilantro leaves
- 1 small purple onion, finely chopped

The Dressing

- ½ cup sesame oil
- ¼ balsamic vinegar
- 2 tablespoons light soy
- 1 tablespoon honey
- 2 tablespoons minced ginger
- 1 tablespoon toasted sesame seeds

TIP: to make it more of a meal, you can add shrimp or chicken to this wonderful refreshing salad or even a hard-boil egg!

PREPARATION

1. Peel and cut your cucumbers into medallions about ¼ inch thick, and place it in a large salad bowl. Toss in the finely chopped scallion, cilantro and purple onion.
2. In a smaller mixing bowl, whisk together the dressing ingredients and drizzle just enough into your cucumber salad to coat everything. Toss well.
3. To serve: spoon your cucumber salad into salad bowls, sprinkle with extra toasted sesame seeds and enjoy!

Thai Noodle Salad with Baby Shrimps

COOK TIME
5-8 MIN
PREP TIME
10 MIN
SERVINGS
2 SERVINGS

INGREDIENTS

- 2 cups baby shrimp, rinsed and drained
- 1 cup corn tidbits
- 1 large purple onion, thinly sliced
- 1 long cucumber, peeled and sliced into thin medallions
- ½ bunch of kale, washed with stems cut, leaves cut into strips
- 1 stalk green scallion, julienned
- 2 cups Vermicelli Noodles (they usually come in a large red package and in squares of sixes, 1 square is roughly 1 cup)

The Dressing

- ½ cup sesame oil
- ¼ cup light soy sauce
- ¼ cup rice wine vinegar
- 1 tablespoon honey
- 1 teaspoon minced garlic
- 1 teaspoon minced ginger
- Fresh pepper to serve
- ¼ cup crushed peanuts

PREPARATION

1. Bring to a boil, a small pot of water, once boiling add in your Vermicelli Noodles and cook until soft on medium heat, roughly 8 minutes. Once cooked drain the noodles over a sieve and put it back into the pot with some ice water. Set aside.

2. Bring to a boil another small pot of water and cook your shrimp in it. Cook for about 2 minutes. Drain with sieve and add it into the ice water bath of your Vermicelli Noodles.

3. In a small mixing bowl whisk together the dressing ingredients. Set aside.

4. In a large salad bowl toss together the corn, sliced onion, sliced cucumbers, and kale. Drain your shrimp and Vermicelli Noodles and toss it with your salad ingredients, drizzle the dressing and toss evenly. To serve: plate your noodle salad, add a sprinkle of the julienned scallions and crushed peanuts and a crack of fresh pepper. Serve with lime wedges.

Taco Salad with Tomato Parsley Dressing

COOK TIME
10-15 MIN
PREP TIME
15 MIN
SERVINGS
2-4 SERVINGS

INGREDIENTS

Taco Seasoning

- ½ tablespoon chili powder
- ¼ teaspoon garlic powder
- ¼ teaspoon onion powder
- ¼ teaspoon pepper flakes
- ¼ teaspoon paprika
- ¼ teaspoon ground cumin
- 1 teaspoon dark soy sauce

- 1 pound ground beef
- 1 tablespoon sesame oil
- 1 cup canned black beans
- 2 cups cherry tomatoes cut in half
- 2 romaine lettuce hearts, washed and shredded
- 2 celery stalks, diced
- 2 stalks green scallion, julienned
- 1 cup shredded sharp cheddar
- 1 cup sour cream
- 1 ½ cup roughly crushed Doritos chips

The Dressing

- 1 cup tomato juice
- 1 cup finely chopped parsley leaves
- 2 teaspoons minced shallots
- 1 teaspoon olive oil
- ½ teaspoon salt
- ½ teaspoon pepper

PREPARATION

1. In a large mixing bowl, season your ground beef with the taco seasoning and set aside. In another small bowl, whisk together the dressing and set aside.

2. Heat up a non-stick skillet over medium heat, once hot add the sesame oil and seasoned beef, sauté until cooked, roughly 10-15 minutes. Then add in the beans and cook for another 5 minutes. Once cooked drain the oil and let the meat and beans cool in a bowl.

3. Combine the cherry tomatoes, shredded lettuce, celery, scallion and cheddar in a large salad bowl, then toss in the crushed Doritos. Once your beef has cooled toss with the salad. To serve: plate your salad into bowls with a drizzle of the dressing and a dollop of the sour cream.

Chilled Tofu with Ginger Sesame Dressing

COOK TIME
10 MIN
PREP TIME
15 MIN
SERVINGS
2 SERVINGS

INGREDIENTS

- 250 grams of medium firm tofu (most packaged tofu come in a rectangle shaped plastic box sitting in water, this is enough to feed 2 people as a light appetizer)
- 1 green scallion stalk, julienned
- ½ cup baby radishes, thinly sliced
- 2 cups boiling hot water (careful when handling it)

The Dressing

- ½ cup sesame oil
- ¼ balsamic vinegar
- 2 tablespoons light soy
- 1 tablespoon honey
- 2 tablespoons minced ginger
- 1 tablespoon toasted sesame seeds

PREPARATION

1. To prep your tofu, drain the water from the package and place the tofu on a flat plate, and place the plate in your clean empty kitchen sink. Slowly pour the boiling water over your tofu this will blanch your tofu. Let it cool for 2 minutes, then drain the warm water from the plate.

2. Cut your tofu cube in half and place each half in separate serving bowls. Refrigerate it while you make your dressing.

3. In a small mixing bowl whisk together your dressing, when ready to serve, evenly distribute the baby radishes and scallions on top of your tofu, and then drizzle the dressing over everything. Serve immediately.

Surf and Turf Cobb Salad with Blue Cheese Dressing

COOK TIME
1 HOUR
PREP TIME
15 MIN
SERVINGS
4 SERVINGS

INGREDIENTS

- 1 pound skirt steak
- 1 teaspoon salt
- 1 teaspoon pepper
- 1 teaspoon sesame oil
- 2 cups baby shrimp, rinsed and drained
- 2 avocado, pitted and sliced
- 1 ½ cups corn tidbits
- 2 cups cherry tomatoes cut in halves
- 2 romaine lettuce hearts, washed and shredded
- 2 eggs, hardboiled, peeled and cut into slices
- 1 cucumber, peeled and sliced
- 1 cup shredded sharp cheddar
- 2 green scallions, julienned

The Dressing

- 1 cup mayo
- ½ cup sour cream
- ¼ cup buttermilk
- 1tablespoon Worcestershire sauce
- 1 cup crumbled blue cheese
- 1 teaspoon salt
- 1 teaspoon black pepper
- 2 tablespoon chives, finely chopped

PREPARATION

1. Season your steak with the salt and pepper, heat up a non-stick frying pan. Add in the sesame oil and fry your skirt steak on medium-low heat for 10 minutes each side.

2. Once cooked (medium-rare) set aside and let it rest. Then cut into slices, and set aside.

3. Bring to a boil a small pot of water, once boiling add the shrimp and let it cook for 5 minutes. Once cooked drain and set aside.

4. In a large mixing bowl, whisk together the dressing ingredients and set aside.

5. Start layering your ingredients: In a large serving plate, cover it with a layer of shredded romaine lettuce. Then layer the rest of your ingredients across the plate

over the lettuce starting with the shrimp and skirt steak in the middle of the plate.

6. Once it's all layered, sprinkle the green scallions over everything and drizzle the dressing over your Surf and Turf Cobb Salad.

Notes

TIP: HAVE FUN WITH YOUR SALAD! SWITCH IT UP BY SUBSTIUTING THE LISTED VEGETABLES WITH ONES THAT ARE SEASON, OR ADD IN YOUR FAVORITES. KEEP IT INTERESTING BY MIXING IN FRUIT, LIKE PINEAPPLES OR MANDARIN ORANGES, FOR A POP OF SWEETNESS!

HOMEMADE SOUPS & STEWS

Hearty Soups and Stews – Homemade Goodness

Vegetable Stew with Barley

COOK TIME
30 MIN
PREP TIME
20 MIN
SERVINGS
6 SERVINGS

INGREDIENTS

- 6 tomatoes, diced
- 2 large carrots, cut into bite size pieces
- 3 potatoes cut into chunks
- 4 celery stalks cut into bite size pieces
- 2 cups of sliced white mushrooms
- 1 large onion, diced
- 6 cups vegetable stock (or beef/chicken stock)
- ½ cup red wine or rice wine (red wine is preferred)
- 1 cup pearl barley
- 3 gloves garlic, minced
- 1 tablespoon dried parsley flakes
- 1 tablespoon dried thyme
- 1 bay leaf

PREPARATION

1. In a non-stick pan add a drizzle of olive oil and quickly sauté the white mushrooms with the minced garlic and onions until golden brown (2-3 minutes on medium heat) then add in the red wine and cook for another minute. Set aside.

2. In medium soup pot bring to a boil your vegetable stock, once boiling add in your tomatoes, carrots, potatoes, and celery and let it cook for 20 minutes, stirring intermittently.

3. Then add in the mushrooms and barley, gently stir them into the vegetable stew. Add salt and pepper to taste and let it cook on medium for another 10 to 15 minutes. If it's too thick, add another cup of vegetable stock. Once everything is soften, then you can turn off the heat and serve with fresh baked biscuits.

Notes

Chicken Butternut Squash Soup with Orzo

COOK TIME
30 MIN
PREP TIME
20 MIN
SERVINGS
4 SERVINGS

PLEASE NOTE: THE RECIPE REQUIRES A BLENDER TO PUREE THE SOUP. YOU CAN ALSO PREPARE THE BUTTERNUT SQUASH A FEW DAYS AHEAD AND STORE IT IN APPROPRIATE PORTIONS AND KEEP IN FREEZER UNTIL NEEDED.

INGREDIENTS

- 1 ½ pounds of fresh already baked butternut squash, peeled and cubed
- 1 tomato diced
- 3 tablespoons butter
- 1 onion, diced
- 1 garlic clove, minced
- ½ cup celery, diced
- ½ cup carrots, diced
- ½ liter chicken broth
- 2 tablespoon red pepper flakes
- 2 tablespoon dried parsley flakes
- ¼ teaspoon freshly ground black pepper
- 1 cup orzo, cooked
- 1 cup chicken breast, seasoned, cooked and diced

PREPARATION

1. Heat up the butter in a medium sized non-stick soup then sauté the following ingredients for 2 minutes:

- 1 onion, diced
- 1 garlic clove, minced
- ½ cup celery, diced
- ½ cup carrots, diced

2. Then add the chicken broth and bring to a boil on high heat. Once boiling, turn it to medium low and add the squash, diced tomato, red pepper flakes, parsley flakes and ground black pepper. Let it cook for 15 minutes. This will soften all your vegetables.

3. Once cooked ladle the butternut squash soup mixture into your blender. Blend until mixture is nice and smooth.

4. Then add it back to your soup pot along with your cooked chicken breast and orzo. Bring it back to a boil for another 15 minutes. Taste and season with salt and pepper accordingly.
5. Serve with fresh dinner rolls and butter on the side.

How to Prepare your Butternut Squash

1. Cut the butternut squash in half and use a spoon to spoon out all the seeds and then wash and rinse over cold running water.

2. Wrap each half in tinfoil, make sure it's fully covered and sealed with the tinfoil. Then preheat your oven to 350 F and bake on the middle rack for 45 minutes to 1 hour. Let it cool, it should be soft enough for you to scoop out the meat with a spoon.

3. Then cut into cubes and keep refrigerated until ready to use.

Notes

Mama's Homey Fish Stew

COOK TIME
30-35 MIN
PREP TIME
15 MIN
SERVINGS
6 SERVINGS

INGREDIENTS

- 2-3 pounds of fresh cod cut into thick strips
- 2 tablespoon sesame oil
- 1 tablespoon white pepper
- 1 tablespoon of salt
- 5 cups of chicken broth
- 1 cup clam juice
- 1 cup heavy cream
- 1 small purple onion diced
- 3 medium size potatoes peeled and diced
- ½ cup white mushroom sliced
- 2 tablespoon dry parsley flakes

PREPARATION

1. In large mixing bowl marinate following and set aside:
- 2-3 pounds of cod
- 2 tablespoon sesame oil
- 1 tablespoon white pepper
- 1 tablespoon of salt

2. In a large soup pot bring to a boil on high heat:
- 5 cups of chicken broth
- 1 cup clam juice

3. Once boiling, stir in the following, and let it simmer on medium heat for 20 minutes or until the potatoes have softened up:
- potatoes
- 1 small purple onion diced
- 3 medium size potatoes peeled and diced
- ½ cup sliced white mushrooms.

4. After the 20 minutes, add in your fish mixture, parsley flakes and heavy cream. Let everything simmer for another 10 to 15 minutes, stirring periodically. If you prefer a thicker stew add a swirl of flour and cook for another 2 minutes. Your stew is cooked when your fish has turned a solid white color. Taste and adjust the salt and pepper seasoning accordingly. Serve with warm dinner rolls and garden salad.

New England Clam Chowder

COOK TIME
25-30 MIN
PREP TIME
15 MIN
SERVINGS
2-4 SERVINGS

INGREDIENTS

- 12-24 fresh clams (or 11 oz. strained frozen or canned clams)
- 2 cups Clam Juice
- 3 cups chicken stock
- ½ cup white wine
- 1 cup, smoked and cured bacon
- 1 medium onion, finely chopped
- 1 teaspoon sea salt
- ¼ teaspoon white pepper
- 2 medium russet potatoes, cubed
- 1 bay leaf
- 1 sprig thyme
- 1 pinch, red pepper flakes
- 1 tablespoon dried parsley flakes
- 1 cup milk
- 1 cup cream
- 1 tablespoon cornstarch mixed with 2 tablespoons of water

PREPARATION

1. Prepare the clams, if fresh wash and scrub thoroughly set aside in a cold water bath. If canned, drain and set aside.

2. In a large non-stick soup pot sauté the bacon and onion with sea salt and white pepper for about 5 minutes, then add in the clam juice, chicken stock and white wine. Stir to combine, then add in the potatoes, bay leaf, thyme, red pepper flakes, parsley flakes, bring to a boil on medium heat. Once boiling add in the potatoes. Let everything cook on medium heat for 20 minutes. Drain your fresh clams and add it to your pot along with the cream, give it a gently stir to combine. Cook on medium heat for another 10 minutes, then stir in the milk.

3. Check thickness of the chowder, if it's on the thin side slowly stir in the cornstarch mixture until at your desired thickness (bring to a boil again for about 5 minutes).

4. Serve in individual bowls with warm bread or soup crackers

Chicken Pot Pie Stew

COOK TIME
30 MIN
PREP TIME
15 MIN
SERVINGS
6-8 SERVINGS

PLEASE NOTE: THE RECIPE REQUIRES A PRESSURE COOKER POT. THIS SOUP FREEZES VERY WELL, YOU CAN MAKE IT IN LARGE BATCHES AND FREEZE ACCORDING TO DESIRED SERVING SIZE.

INGREDIENTS

- 4 cups of chicken breast cut into cubes
- 2 large sized russet potatoes, cut into large dices
- 1 large onion, chopped into chunks
- 2 cups of frozen mixed vegetable bits (carrots, peas, corn tidbits)
- Salt and pepper to taste
- 8 cups of chicken broth
- 2 cups heavy cream (or milk)
- 2 tablespoon flour

PREPARATION

1. Once timer goes off carefully release pressure and remove lid. Take out the chicken breasts to a plate, let it cool then cut the chicken breasts into small pieces and put it back into the pot.

2. Add the following ingredients into your pressure cooker pot:

- 4 cups of chicken breast cut into cubes
- 2 large sized russet potatoes, cut into smaller chunks
- 1 large onion, chopped into chunks
- 2 cups of frozen mixed vegetable bits (carrots, peas, corn tidbits)
- 8 cups of chicken broth

3. Lock lid and cook on High for 20 minutes. Set timer. Once timer goes off, carefully release pressure naturally, give the stew a quick stir and add 1 pinch and one crack of fresh pepper. Stir in the heavy cream and the 2 tablespoons of flour into the stew and mix well.

4. Lock lid again and cook on High for another 10 minutes. Set timer. Once timer goes off, release pressure naturally. Season with more salt and pepper to taste and serve with crusty bread or your favorite crackers.

Creamy Potato Cheese Soup

COOK TIME
15 MIN
PREP TIME
10 MIN
SERVINGS
4-6 SERVINGS

PLEASE NOTE: THE RECIPE REQUIRES A BLENDER TO PUREE THE SOUP AND PRESSURE COOKING POT. THIS SOUP FREEZES VERY WELL. YOU CAN MAKE IT IN LARGE BATCHES AND FREEZE ACCORDING TO DESIRED SERVING SIZE.

INGREDIENTS

- 4 large russet potatoes, peeled and cut into 1 inch cubes
- 4 small onions, chopped into chunks
- 2 cups of cauliflower heads, diced
- 4 cups milk
- 6 cups chicken stock
- 2 teaspoons sea salt
- 2 teaspoon white pepper
- ½ teaspoon oregano
- ½ teaspoon garlic powder
- 3 cups white cheddar cheese, grated
- ½ cup finely chopped parsley leaves for garnish

PREPARATION

1. Put potatoes, onions, cauliflower, salt, white pepper, oregano, garlic powder and chicken stock in pressure cooker. Cook on High for 20 minutes. Set timer.

2. Once timer goes off, release pressure naturally and carefully remove lid and allow the potatoes to cool. Once cooled, spoon everything into a blender, and blend until smooth.

3. Add it back into your pressure cooking pot and bring it back to a boil, once boiling add in the milk, stirring constantly, then add in the cheese and stir until melted. Season to taste.

4. Serve immediately with parsley leaves and fresh warm dinner rolls or toasted croissants.

PASTAS NOODLES

Easy Quintessential Lunches & Dinners

Pasta with Meat Sauce

COOK TIME
25 MIN
PREP TIME
15 MIN
SERVINGS
4 SERVINGS

INGREDIENTS

- 6 cups tomato sauce
- 2 cups tomato paste
- 2 cups chicken stock
- 2 pounds ground beef
- 1 small red bell pepper, finely diced
- 1 onion, minced
- 2 cloves of garlic, minced
- 2 teaspoons sea salt
- 2 teaspoons pepper
- 1 tablespoon sriracha
- ½ tablespoon oregano
- ½ tablespoon dried parsley flakes
- 2 bay leaves
- 1 tablespoon sesame oil
- 4 cups of cooked pasta of your choice (this is to serve with the sauce – freeze the rest for future meals)

PREPARATION

1. In a large mixing bowl, marinate your beef with the tomato paste, salt and pepper, sriracha, oregano and dried parsley flakes. Set aside.

2. In a non-stick sauce pot or pan with high sides: heat up the sesame oil over medium heat and sauté your onion and garlic for about 1-2 minutes then add in your bell peppers and sauté for another minute. Add in your beef mixture and let it brown for about 15 minutes over medium heat.

3. Then add in the tomato sauce and chicken stock, stir with a wooden spoon to combine, then add in your bay leaves. Let your meat sauce simmer on medium heat for another 10 minutes. This will reduce some of the liquid and thicken up your meat sauce.

4. After the 10 minutes taste the sauce and season accordingly.

5. Serve it over your favorite pasta or use it as a dipping sauce for crusty bread.

6. This sauce goes great with any type of pasta and it freezes very well for up to 2 weeks.

Macaroni in a Creamy Lemon Sauce

COOK TIME
20 MIN
PREP TIME
15 MIN
SERVINGS
4-6 SERVINGS

INGREDIENTS

- 4 cups dried macaroni
- 4 cups chicken stock
- 2 teaspoons sea salt
- 4 ounces cream cheese, cubed
- 2 cups shredded white cheddar
- ½ cup shredded white cheddar (garnish)
- 1 ½ cup evaporated milk
- 2 tablespoons lemon juice (you can always add a little bit more, if you prefer a more tart taste)
- 1 teaspoon fresh grated lemon zest
- 2 tablespoons dried parsley (optional)
- Fresh cracked pepper and sea salt to taste

PREPARATION

1. This is a one pot pasta, you will need a medium or large non-stick sauce pot with a lid. Submerge your macaroni with the chicken stock in the pot (this will ensure the pasta will cook evenly). Sprinkle the sea salt evenly over your macaroni and a small drizzle of olive oil.

2. And cook on medium heat covered with lid on for 15 minutes. Set a timer. Once your timer goes off check your pasta, the liquid should be cooked down.

3. Use a wooden spoon to stir in the evaporated milk and cream cheese. Bring to a boil and stir until the cream cheese has melted. Stir in the 2 cups of white cheddar and lemon juice along with the parsley flakes. Bring to a simmer on medium heat for another 5 minutes. Turn off heat, remove the pot from the stove and sprinkle in the lemon zest. Taste to adjust the seasoning to your desire. Serve immediately and garnish with the remainder of the white cheddar and fresh cracked pepper. Serve with your favorite salad.

Linguine with Sun-Dried Tomatoes and Brie

COOK TIME
20-25 MIN
PREP TIME
15 MIN
SERVINGS
4 SERVINGS

INGREDIENTS

- 6 inches dried linguine, broken in half
- 1 cup packed fresh basil leaves
- ½ cup sliced oil-packed sun-dried tomatoes
- 3 large garlic cloves, minced
- 4 ½ cups chicken stock
- 2 tablespoons sesame oil
- 1 tablespoon sea salt
- 1 teaspoon red pepper flakes
- Freshly ground black pepper, to taste
- 8 ounces brie cheese, rind removed and torn into pieces
- Good-quality olive oil, for serving

PREPARATION

1. This is a one pot pasta, you will need a medium or large non-stick sauce pot with a lid. Combine the linguine, basil, roasted sun-dried tomatoes, and garlic into the pot, then add the chicken broth, sesame oil, salt, red pepper flakes, and evenly sprinkle a generous amount of black pepper over everything. Bring to a boil first, then cover with lid and cook on medium heat for 20 minutes. Set a timer.

2. Once timer goes off, turn heat to medium low and use tongs to stir the pasta and taste it. Once the pasta is at your desired texture, add in the brie and toss until creamy and melted – roughly 5 minutes.

3. Turn off heat and add in the fresh basil along with a swirl of olive oil. Toss to coat everything with the oil and basil leaves.

4. Serve immediately with crusty baguettes and a fresh garden salad.

Creamy Mixed Mushroom Fettucine

COOK TIME
20 MIN
PREP TIME
15 MIN
SERVINGS
4 SERVINGS

INGREDIENTS

- 6 inches dried fettucine
- ½ cup white mushrooms, sliced
- 1 cup Portobello mushrooms, sliced
- 1 cup cremini mushrooms, sliced
- 2 garlic cloves, minced
- 1 small shallot, minced
- 2 tablespoon sesame oil
- 1 tablespoon sea salt
- 1 tablespoon white pepper
- 1 tablespoon dried oregano
- 2 tablespoon dried parsley flakes
- ½ cup heavy cream
- 250g cream cheese, cut into small cubes
- 1 cup Fresh grated Monterey Jack Cheese

PREPARATION

1. Bring a medium sized pot of water to boil – you will use this to cook your fettucine. Once boiling, add in your pasta and let it cook on medium heat for 10 to 15 minutes. Set a timer.

2. In a non-stick frying pan heat up the sesame oil and sauté all the mushrooms with the garlic and shallot, sea salt, pepper, oregano, and parsley flakes for about 10 minutes, sweating out as much of the liquid as you can in the mushrooms.

3. Then add in the heavy cream. Stir to combine. Then add in the cream cheese, keep stirring until it's melted. By this time your pasta should be done. Drain the liquid and add the fettucine to your mushroom sauce. Turn off the heat and using tongs, toss the fettucine in the mushroom sauce until it's well mixed.

4. Serve immediately on individual plates, sprinkle each plate with the Monterey Jack cheese and fresh cracked pepper and sea salt. Serve with your favorite garden salad or crusty bread.

Pepperoni Pizza Rigatoni

COOK TIME
25-30 MIN
PREP TIME
15 MIN
SERVINGS
2-4 SERVINGS

INGREDIENTS

- 5 ground Italian sausages, sliced thinly
- 2 tablespoon olive oil
- ½ cup pepperoni, sliced in half
- ½ cup pepperoni for layering
- 4 cups dried rigatoni
- 4 cups of tomato sauce (use your favorite)
- 1 cup tomato paste
- 2 cups shredded mozzarella cheese
- Salt and pepper to taste

PREPARATION

1. Fill a medium pot with water and bring it to a boil. Add your rigatoni and olive oil into the boiling water and let it cook over medium heat for 15 minutes. Set a timer. Meanwhile, preheat your oven to 350 F.

2. Once your pasta is cooked drain the liquid, you will need a deep baking dish. In the baking dish add a layer of the rigatoni, then a layer of the Italian sausages and pepperoni, a layer of tomato sauce mixed with the tomato paste and a layer of the mozzarella. Keep layering until you have used up all your ingredients.

3. Once you are finished layering make sure you add extra cheese and pepperoni to your top layer. Bake in middle rack for 15 minutes. Set timer. Once timer goes off, the cheese should be melted and a nice golden brown color. Serve immediately with soup or salad.

Notes

CURRIES
CHILIES

Hot & Spicy for the Pros and Novices

Easy Chili Dog Sauce

COOK TIME
20 MIN
PREP TIME
15 MIN
SERVINGS
4-6 SERVINGS

PLEASE NOTE: THE RECIPE REQUIRES A PRESSURE COOKER POT.

INGREDIENTS

- 1 pound ground beef
- 1 small onion, minced
- 2 cups of canned Mexican pinto beans
- 2 cup beef stock
- ½ cup tomato paste
- 2 tablespoon Dijon
- 1 tablespoon chili oil
- 1 tablespoon chili powder
- 2 tablespoon Worcestershire sauce
- 1 teaspoon sea salt
- 1 teaspoon black pepper
- Fresh grated cheddar to serve

PREPARATION

1. In large mixing bowl combine the following ingredients with your ground beef and set aside:

- 2 tablespoon Dijon
- 1 tablespoon chili oil
- 1 tablespoon chili powder
- 2 tablespoon Worcestershire sauce
- 1 teaspoon sea salt
- 1 teaspoon black pepper

2. In your pressure cooking pot sauté the minced onion with a drizzle of olive oil for about 2 minutes, then stir in the pinto beans, beef stock and tomato paste. Lock lid and cook on High for 10 minutes. Set timer. Once timer goes off release pressure naturally.

3. Stir in your beef mixture into the pot, lock lid and cook on High again for another 10 minutes. Set timer. Once timer goes off, release pressure naturally and give the sauce a stir once more before serving. Adjust the seasoning to taste.

1. Serve over warm hot dogs with a sprinkle of fresh grated cheddar and a side of pickles.

Easy Coconut Seafood Curry

COOK TIME
15-20 MIN
PREP TIME
15 MIN
SERVINGS
4-6 SERVINGS

PLEASE NOTE: THE RECIPE REQUIRES A PRESSURE COOKER POT.

INGREDIENTS

- 2 tablespoons sesame oil
- 1 onion, thinly sliced
- 1 garlic clove, crushed
- 2cm piece ginger, grated
- 2 tablespoons mild curry paste
- 1 tablespoon tomato puree
- 10 prawns, peeled, tails intact
- 1 pound Manila clams, scrubbed and washed
- 2 cans coconut milk
- 1 cup chicken stock
- 2 tablespoons lime juice
- 2 tablespoons chopped coriander leaves

PREPARATION

1. In large mixing bowl combine the following and set aside:
   - 2 tablespoons sesame oil
   - 1 onion, thinly sliced
   - 1 garlic clove, crushed
   - 2cm piece ginger, grated
   - 2 tablespoons mild curry paste
   - 1 tablespoon tomato puree
   - 10 prawns, peeled, tails intact
   - 1 pound Manila clams, scrubbed and washed
2. Set pressure cooker on High and add the chicken stock and coconut milk and the seafood mixture. Cook on High for 15 minutes. Set timer.
3. Once timer goes off release pressure. Give it a good stir and adjust seasoning to taste, and serve with coriander leaves and lime juice.

Notes

Easy Jumbo Shrimp Curry

COOK TIME
15-20 MIN
PREP TIME
15 MIN
SERVINGS
4 SERVINGS

PLEASE NOTE: THE RECIPE REQUIRES A PRESSURE COOKER POT.

INGREDIENTS

- 1 pound frozen jumbo shrimp, thawed and peeled
- Salt and White Pepper to taste
- 1 tablespoon dried parsley
- 1 tablespoon Sesame oil
- 1 tablespoon rice wine
- 1 small onion, diced
- 1 green pepper, diced
- 1 tablespoon olive oil

For the Curry (simplified version)

- ½ tablespoon grated fresh ginger
- 1 diced red Thai chili pepper
- 2 cloves minced garlic
- 1 can of chicken broth
- 1 can of coconut milk
- 1 cup of yellow curry powder
- 1 tablespoon cornstarch + cold water

PREPARATION

1. In a large mixing bowl marinate your shrimp with the following ingredients then set aside: Couple pinches of salt and white pepper, dried parsley, sesame oil, and rice wine.

2. In another bowl whisk together the chicken broth and coconut milk then slowly add the curry powder. Whisk well. Then add the minced garlic, Thai chili pepper and ginger. Set aside.

3. Turn pressure cooker on high and sauté the onion and green pepper with olive oil, once onion is tender. Add the curry mixture and add the marinated shrimp. Cover and lock lid and cook on High for 15 minutes. Set timer. Once timer goes off. Release pressure naturally and give the curry a good stir. Only add in the cornstarch mixture if it's not at your desired thickness.

4. Season with salt and pepper to taste. Serve over jasmine rice or Asian egg noodles. It's great for dipping crusty baguettes too!

Easy Indian Butter Chicken

COOK TIME
20 MIN
PREP TIME
10 MIN
SERVINGS
6-8 SERVINGS

PLEASE NOTE: THE RECIPE REQUIRES A PRESSURE COOKER POT.

INGREDIENTS

- 8 pieces of small chicken drumsticks
- 4 large tomatoes diced
- 4 small red Thai chili peppers, chopped
- 2 tablespoons fresh ginger, peeled and chopped into thin slices
- 1 cup of tomato sauce
- ½ cup tomato paste
- ½ cup melted butter
- 2 teaspoons ground cumin
- ½ tablespoon paprika
- 2 teaspoons sea salt
- ½ cup heavy cream
- ¼ cup Greek yogurt
- 2 tablespoons garam masala
- 2 tablespoons cornstarch
- 2 tablespoons water
- ¼ cup firmly packed minced cilantro leaves and stems

PREPARATION

1. Put tomatoes, tomato sauce, tomato paste, Thai chili peppers and ginger in a blender or food processor and pulse into a fine puree.

2. Add butter to pressure cooker and once the butter begins to foam, add the chicken drumsticks and cook until the skin is a nice golden brown – about 10 minutes.

3. Season chicken with sea salt and paprika. Use tongs to evenly coat the chicken with the spices. Once coated, remove the chicken from the pressure cooker and set aside.

4. In the same pressure cooker, add ground cumin to the left over butter and chicken fat in the pot, stirring quickly.

5. When the cumin is fragrant, add the tomato mixture from your blender, a pinch of salt, cream, and yogurt.

6. Add the chicken drumsticks back into the pot and gently stir to coat the drumsticks with the sauce.

7. Cover the pot and lock lid. Set the timer for 20 minutes and cook on high.

8. When timer goes off, release pressure naturally according to your pressure cooker instructions and stir in the garam masala.

9. In a separate small bowl, whisk together cornstarch and cold water to make a slurry. Slowly pour the cornstarch slurry into the sauce. Bring the sauce back to a boil for about 5 minutes. The cornstarch slurry will thicken the sauce.

10. Turn off pressure cooker and stir in some finely chopped cilantro. Serve with rice and naan on the side for dipping.

Notes

Easy Hot Red Fish Curry

COOK TIME
10 MIN
PREP TIME
10 MIN
SERVINGS
4 SERVINGS

PLEASE NOTE: THE RECIPE REQUIRES A PRESSURE COOKER POT.

INGREDIENTS

- 2 pounds of red snapper filet cut into thick strips
- 1 tablespoon sea salt and white pepper
- ¼ cup grated fresh ginger
- 1 tablespoon soy sauce
- 2 tablespoon chili oil
- 1 tablespoon Sesame oil
- 1 tablespoon rice wine
- 1 small onion, diced
- 2 large tomatoes diced
- ½ tablespoon honey

For the Red Curry

- 3 diced red Thai chili pepper
- 2 cloves minced garlic
- 4 cups tomato sauce
- 2 cups of chicken broth
- 1 can of coconut milk
- ½ cup of red curry powder
- One cup chopped cilantro leaves
- 1 tablespoon cornstarch + cold water (this is used to thicken the curry only if it's not thick enough)

PREPARATION

1. In a large mixing bowl marinate the snapper with the salt and white pepper, grated ginger, chili oil, sesame oil and rice wine. Set aside to marinate while you prepare your other ingredients.

2. In a medium mixing bowl combine the onion, tomatoes, soy sauce and honey. Set aside. In another mixing bowl whisk together the curry ingredients and set aside. In your pressure cooking pot bring to a boil the whisked curry sauce ingredients and the onion and tomato mixture.

3. Once boiling add your snapper pieces into the pressure cooking pot. Lock lid and cook on High for 15 minutes. Set timer. Once timer goes off release pressure naturally.

4. Use a wooden spoon and gently stir the curry. Stir in the cornstarch mixture slowly, then stir in the cilantro leaves. Let the heat in the pressure cooking pot naturally cook the leaves for about 2 minutes.

5. Serve immediately with jasmine rice or any type of pasta.

Notes

TIP: A PRESSURE COOKER POT, OR AN "INSTANT POT", IS A GREAT INVESTMENT. IT CUTS DOWN ON COOKING TIME, HELPS FOOD RETAIN MOST OF THEIR NUTRIENTS, AND MOST MEALS CAN BE MADE ALL IN ONE POT. BUT IF YOU DO NOT HAVE ACCESS TO A PRESSURE COOKER POT, A THICK BOTTOMED POT WILL WORK AS WELL. MAKE SURE TO INCREASE COOKING TIME ACCORDINGLY AND KEEP A CLOSE EYE ON THE CONTENTS!

POULTRY LOVERS

Spicy Saucy BBQ Wings

COOK TIME
30 MIN
PREP TIME
10 MIN
SERVINGS
4-6 SERVINGS

INGREDIENTS

- 20 chicken wings, arm of the wing intact
- Salt and pepper (used to season wings)
- 3 tablespoon sesame oil
- ½ cup tomato paste
- 4 tablespoons soy sauce
- 4 tablespoons white vinegar
- 1 cup red wine
- ½ cup chili hot sauce

PREPARATION

1. In a large bowl, toss the wings generously with salt and pepper and sesame oil and soy sauce.
2. Preheat oven to 375 F and cover a baking sheet in tinfoil. Evenly layout your chicken wings and cook on middle rack of the hot oven for 30 minutes. Set a timer. Once your times goes off. Take it out and let it cool for a couple of minutes before serving.
3. Serve with your favorite cucumber slices and celery sticks.

Spicy Thai Hot Wings

COOK TIME
30 MIN
PREP TIME
10 MIN
SERVINGS
4-6 SERVINGS

INGREDIENTS

- 20 chicken wings, arm of the wing intact
- 4 cloves minced garlic
- 1 tablespoon black pepper
- 1 tablespoon palm sugar, grated
- 1 tablespoon soy sauce
- 2 tablespoon sesame oil
- 2 tablespoon lime juice
- 1 tablespoon chili garlic sauce to taste

PREPARATION

1. In a large bowl, toss the wings generously with salt and pepper and sesame oil and soy sauce.
2. Preheat oven to 375 F and cover a baking sheet in tinfoil. Evenly layout your chicken wings and

cook on middle rack of the hot oven for 30 minutes. Set a timer. Once your times goes off. Take it out and let it cool for a couple of minutes before serving. Serve with your favorite cucumber slices and celery sticks.

Sticky Sriracha Honey Wings

COOK TIME
30 MIN
PREP TIME
10 MIN
SERVINGS
4-6 SERVINGS

INGREDIENTS

- 20 chicken wings, arm of the wing intact
- Salt and pepper (used to season wings)
- 1 tablespoon sesame oil
- 3 tablespoons melted butter
- 1 cup Sriracha Sauce
- 1 cup honey
- 1 tablespoon rice wine
- 1 teaspoon soy sauce
- 1 teaspoon hoisin sauce
- 2 tablespoons chopped cilantro

PREPARATION

1. In a large bowl, toss the wings generously with salt and pepper and sesame oil. Then add the butter, Sriracha, honey, soy sauce, rice wine, and hoisin sauce. Coat evenly then set aside.

2. Preheat oven to 375 F and cover a baking sheet in tinfoil. Evenly layout your chicken wings and cook on middle rack of the hot oven for 30 minutes. Set a timer. Once your times goes off. Take it out and let it cool for a couple of minutes then sprinkle the fresh chopped cilantro before serving.

3. Serve with your favorite cucumber slices and celery sticks.

Notes

Salt and Pepper Chicken Wings

COOK TIME
30 MIN
PREP TIME
10 MIN
SERVINGS
4-6 SERVINGS

INGREDIENTS

- 20 chicken wings, arm of the wing intact
- 2-4 tablespoon of coarse salt
- 6 tablespoon pepper
- 2 tablespoon sesame oil
- Fresh lemon wedges for serving

PREPARATION

1. In mixing bowl mix together all the above ingredients not including the lemon wedges. Make sure each wing is coated with pepper, be generous with the pepper.

2. Preheat oven to 375 F and cover a baking sheet in tinfoil. Evenly layout your chicken wings and cook on middle rack of the hot oven for 30 minutes. Set a timer. Once your times goes off. Take it out and let it cool for a couple of minutes before serving.

3. Serve with the fresh lemon wedges and your favorite cucumber slices and celery sticks.

Chicken Parmesan Meatballs

COOK TIME
40 MIN
PREP TIME
15 MIN
SERVINGS
4 SERVINGS

PLEASE NOTE: THE RECIPE REQUIRES A PRESSURE COOKER POT.

INGREDIENTS

- 1 pound ground chicken
- ½ cup seasoned breadcrumbs
- 1 cup freshly grated Parmesan cheese
- 2 shallots, minced
- 1 garlic clove, minced
- Small handful of chopped parsley
- ¼ teaspoon salt
- ¼ teaspoon pepper
- 1 egg, beaten
- 1 tablespoon olive oil
- 1 can chicken broth
- 2 teaspoons ranch dressing
- 2 ounces cream cheese
- 1 teaspoon lemon juice

PREPARATION

1. In large mixing bowl combine the following:

- 1 pound ground chicken
- ½ cup seasoned breadcrumbs
- 1 cup freshly grated Parmesan cheese
- 2 shallots, minced
- 1 garlic clove, minced
- Small handful of chopped parsley
- ¼ teaspoon salt
- ¼ teaspoon pepper
- 1 egg, beaten
- 1 tablespoon olive oil

2. Once combined, spoon a large tablespoon of the chicken mixture onto your hand and roll the chicken mixture between your palms to form golf ball sized meat balls.

3. Line a large tray or platter with wax paper. Place each meatball on the tray in a single layer – making sure to leave enough space in-between each meatball to keep the meatballs from sticking to each other. Refrigerate the meat balls for at least 30 minutes or overnight.

4. Once the meatballs are ready to cook, heat a skillet on high heat and sear the meatballs in olive oil until the surface has caramelized. Turn off heat and set aside.

5. Set your pressure cooker on high and combine chicken broth, ranch dressing, cream cheese and lemon juice.

6. Place a single layer of the meatballs into pressure cooker. Careful to not over crowd.

7. Cover and lock the lid. Set the time for 30 minutes and cook on high.

8. Once timer goes off, release pressure naturally according to the instructions for your pressure cooker. Ladle a generous serving over your favorite pasta, or serve on a toasted roll to make a hearty meatball sandwich.

Notes

TIP: YOU CAN MAKE A BATCH OF THE MEATBALLS AND COOK THEM IN YOUR PRESSURE COOKER AND FREEZE THEM. MAKE SURE YOU PORTION THEM TO YOUR DESIRED SERVING BEFORE FREEZING. THEY KEEP WELL FOR UP TO 3 WEEKS!

Pineapple and Chicken Lettuce Wrap

COOK TIME
30 MIN
PREP TIME
15 MIN
SERVINGS
4 SERVINGS

INGREDIENTS

- 10 small boneless, skinless, chicken breast
- 2 cups chicken stock
- 1 cup rice wine
- 2 tablespoons white vinegar
- 2 tablespoon sesame oil
- 4 tablespoon dark soy sauce
- 2 tablespoon white pepper
- 2 tablespoon chili flakes
- 3 garlic cloves, minced
- 1 stock of green onion finely chopped
- 1 can of diced pineapples, drained
- 1 head of butter lettuce, peeled with leaves intact and washed, let dry
- Hoisin Sauce for dipping

PREPARATION

1. In large mixing bowl, marinate chicken breast with soy sauce, sesame oil, pepper, chili flakes and garlic. Set aside.

2. In a medium sized soup pot, bring the chicken stock and rice wine to a boil over medium high heat.

3. Once the stock is boiling, add the marinated chicken breast to the pot and let it simmer. Leave the lid ajar to help release steam. Alternatively, you can lay a wooden spoon across the top of the pot to prevent the stock from over-boiling. Set a timer for 25 minutes.

4. Once the timer goes off, check to make sure your chicken breast is fully cooked. If the chicken is still slightly pink, set the timer for an additional five minutes.

5. When the chicken is fully cooked, remove it from the pot and let it cool before shredding.

6. To shred, use two forks to tear the meat until you are left with bite-sized pieces.

7. Place the shredded chicken into a large bowl and add the diced pineapples into a large bowl, along with a tablespoon of Hoisin sauce. Stir in the green onions and its ready to serve.

8. To serve, spoon the chicken and pineapple mixture into the lettuce leaf. Fold up the lettuce leaf like a "taco" shell and dip into the Hoisin sauce.

TIP: HAVING FRIENDS OVER? HAVE A LETTUCE WRAP PARTY! PREP ALL INGREDIENTS AND LAY IT OUT ON A PLATTER WITH SOME WASHED LETTUCE ON THE SIDE. LET YOUR GUESTS ASSEMBLE THEIR OWN WRAPS. SPICE IT UP WITH SOME EXTRA DIPS LIKE SRIRACHA MAYO OR HONEY MUSTARD, AND ADD IN SOME FUN TOPPINGS INTO THE MIX SUCH AS:

- CRUMBLED TORTILLA CHIPS
- DICED CUCUMBERS
- GRILLED CORN

THIS RECIPE SERVES 4, SO MAKE SURE TO DOUBLE UP (OR TRIPLE) THE PORTIONS SO EVERYONE HAS ENOUGH FOR SECONDS AS WELL!

Chicken Tender Strips

COOK TIME
35 MIN
PREP TIME
10 MIN
SERVINGS
4 SERVINGS

INGREDIENTS

- 3 pound chicken tenders cut into strips (this should give you around 6-8 strips of chicken)
- ½ tablespoon salt
- 2 tablespoon pepper
- 1 tablespoon soy sauce
- 1 tablespoon sesame oil
- 1 cup breadcrumbs
- 2 cups panko (Japanese Style breadcrumbs)
- ½ cup flour
- 2eggs

PREPARATION

1. Season chicken strips with the following and set aside:

- 1 tablespoon salt
- 2 tablespoon pepper
- 1 tablespoon soy sauce
- 1 tablespoon sesame oil

2. Toss breadcrumbs and panko with flour, set aside.

3. Beat the eggs and coat your chicken with it, then dip into panko breadcrumb mixture until well coated.

4. Preheat oven to 375 F. Lightly grease your baking sheet with some olive oil. Then lay the strips evenly on your baking sheet and bake in your hot oven in the middle rack for 15 minutes. Set timer. Once timer goes off. Take it out and using tongs, carefully flip each chicken strip oven. Put it back into your oven and bake it again for another 15 minutes. Set timer. Once timer goes off. Turn your oven on Broil at 500 F and let it broil for about 5-8 minutes. You will need to watch it so it does not burn. Broiling will give the chicken strips a darker golden brown color.

5. Serve with your favorite dipping sauce and a sprinkle of fresh pepper and a cucumber salad.

Herbed Chicken Breast with Mustard Dressing

COOK TIME
25 MIN
PREP TIME
10 MIN
SERVINGS
4 SERVINGS

INGREDIENTS

- 2 medium size chicken breasts
- ½ tablespoon salt
- 2 tablespoon onion flakes
- 2 tablespoon dried oregano
- 2 tablespoon dried parsley flakes
- 2 tablespoon garlic powder
- 2 tablespoon sesame oil
- 1 bag of arugula greens

For the Mustard Dressing

- 1 cup Dijon
- 1 ½ cup sour cream
- 1 tablespoon honey
- 1 tablespoon sesame oil
- 1 tablespoon onion flakes
- Fresh cracked pepper and salt to taste
- 1 sprig of fresh green onion, finely sliced

PREPARATION

1. In mixing bowl mix together all the dry ingredients first, not including the chicken breasts and arugula greens. Once the spices are mixed coat your chicken breast with it and let it marinate for 10 minutes.

2. In another smaller mixing bowl mix together the Mustard Dressing ingredients and keep chilled before serving.

3. Preheat oven to 375 F and lay the chicken breasts in a lightly greased baking sheet and bake for 15 minutes. Set timer. Once timer goes off, flip the breast and bake for another 15 minutes. Set timer.

4. Once timer goes off, plate it on top of the arugula greens and serve with a dollop of the Mustard Dressing.

Spicy Chicken Nuggets

COOK TIME
30-35 MIN
PREP TIME
10 MIN
SERVINGS
4 SERVINGS

INGREDIENTS

- 4 pound chicken breasts cut into nugget size
- ½ tablespoon salt
- 2 tablespoon Shichimi Powder (it's a Japanese Seasoning)
- 2 tablespoon Sriracha sauce
- 2 tablespoon Tabasco sauce (this adds a bit of a tart note to the sauce)
- 1 tablespoon chili oil
- 2 cups bread crumbs mixed with 2 tablespoons of chili flakes

---

PREPARATION

1. In mixing bowl mix together the following and set aside, make sure each nugget is coated with the sauce:

- 4 pound chicken breasts cut into nugget size
- 1 tablespoon salt
- 2 tablespoon Shichimi Powder (Japanese Seasoning)
- 2 tablespoon Sriracha sauce
- 2 tablespoon Tabasco sauce
- 1 tablespoon chili oil

2. Once everything is mixed and seasoned coat each nugget in the breadcrumb mixture. The breadcrumb mixture is a "dry rub" for the nuggets.

3. Preheat Air Fryer to 375 F. Then lightly grease your baking sheet with some olive oil and lay out the nuggets. Bake in middle rack for 20 minutes. Set timer.

4. Once timer goes off, take out the baking sheet and using tongs, flip your chicken nuggets and bake again in the oven for 10 minutes. Set timer. Once timer goes off, set your oven to broil and broil at 500 F for about 5 minutes. Watch your nuggets, make sure it does not burn. Broiling will give you a nice dark golden brown color. Once done broiling, take it out of the oven and let it cool for about 5 minutes before serving.

5. Serve with fresh celery sticks and cucumber slices.

Ultimate Turkey Nacho Sauce

COOK TIME
15 MIN
PREP TIME
10 MIN
SERVINGS
6-8 SERVINGS

INGREDIENTS

- 1 pound ground turkey meat
- 2 tablespoon sesame oil
- 2 tablespoon sea salt
- 2 tablespoon crack pepper
- 2 tablespoon thyme
- 2 tablespoon dried parsley flakes
- 1 small onion, diced
- 1 cup finely diced green bell peppers
- 2 jalapeno peppers cut into thin rounds
- ¼ cup lemon zest (save the wedges for garnish)
- ½ cup black olives
- 1 small bunch of cilantro leaves coarsely cut
- 1 cup of chicken broth
- 2 cups grated sharp cheddar
- Sour cream to serve and a bag of your favorite nachos

PREPARATION

1. In a large mixing bowl, mix together the turkey meat with sesame oil, salt, pepper, thyme and parsley. Set aside.

2. In a medium size soup pot bring to a boil on high heat the 1 cup of chicken broth. Then add in the onion, bell peppers, jalapeno and black olives.

3. Turn the heat to medium and let it simmer for 10 minutes. Then add in your turkey mixture, stir to break apart the meat. Turn heat on high, keep stirring while you cook the turkey meat with the rest of your ingredients, reducing as much of the liquid as possible without drying it out. This will take another 10 to 15 minutes. Once the liquid is reduced, use a slotted spoon to remove your turkey mixture to a bowl – discard the liquid. Set aside the bowl and preheat your oven to 375 F

4. Lightly grease a baking sheet and pour a layer of the nachos onto it. Then top it off with a generous layer of the turkey mixture, and then evenly sprinkle the 2 cups of sharp cheddar over your nachos.

5. Bake in middle rack of your hot oven for about 10 minutes or until the cheese has melted.

6. Take it out, serve immediately. Garnish it with a sprinkle of the cilantro and lemon zest the sour cream and extra cheese and olives!

Notes

TIP: For a richer nacho sauce, swap the broth for cream or milk. There is also no limit to cheese! Customize your sauce by mixing and matching your favorite cheese. Combinations to try:

- **MONTEREY JACK**
- **MOZZARELLA**
- **BLUE CHEESE (IF YOU ARE FEELING ADVENTUROUS)**

MEAT LOVERS

Korean Style Beef Short Ribs

COOK TIME
30 MIN
PREP TIME
15 MIN
SERVINGS
4-6 SERVINGS

PLEASE NOTE: THE RECIPE REQUIRES A PRESSURE COOKER POT.

INGREDIENTS

- 4 pounds bottom roast, cut into cubes
- 2 cups tofu puff (deep fried tofu puffs)
- 1 teaspoon white pepper
- 2 tablespoons sesame oil
- 1 cup beef broth
- ½ cup rice wine
- ½ cup soy sauce
- 5 cloves garlic, minced
- 1 medium onion, diced
- 1 teaspoon fresh grated ginger
- ½ cup gochujang
- ¼ cup mirin
- ¼ cup ketchup
- 2 stalks green onion, julienned for garnish

PREPARATION

1. In a large mixing bowl, whisk together the white pepper, soy sauce, gochujang, mirin and ketchup. Then marinate your beef cubes in it. Set aside.

2. In your pressure cooking pot sauté the minced garlic, onion and grated ginger with the sesame oil, for about 2 minutes. Then add in the beef broth and rice wine. Stir to combine.

3. Now add in your beef with the marinade. Stir to combine. Lock lid and cook on High for 20 minutes. Set timer. Once timer goes off release pressure naturally and add in your tofu puffs. Stir to combine. Lock lid and cook on High again for another 5 minutes. Set timer.

4. Once timer goes off, release pressure naturally, stir to combine. Serve with Korean rice or udon and garnish with the green onions.

Mexican Style Short Ribs

COOK TIME
20 MIN
PREP TIME
15 MIN
SERVINGS
4-6 SERVINGS

INGREDIENTS

- 3 pounds short ribs
- 1 teaspoon sesame oil
- 4 tablespoons soy sauce
- ½ teaspoon cayenne pepper
- 1 teaspoon paprika
- 2 tablespoon chili powder
- 2 tablespoon ground cumin
- 2 teaspoon onion powder
- ½ cup beef stock
- ½ cup red wine

PREPARATION

1. Whisk together the following seasonings into a large mixing bowl:
   - 1 teaspoon sesame oil
   - 4 tablespoons soy sauce
   - ½ teaspoon cayenne pepper
   - 1 teaspoon paprika
   - 2 tablespoon chili powder
   - 2 tablespoon ground cumin
   - 2 teaspoon onion powder

2. Add your ribs into the mixing bowl and marinate for about 10 minutes. (The flavor will be more robust if you marinated it overnight).

3. In a medium sized, soup pot bring to a boil on medium heat the beef stock and red wine, stir to combine. Once boiling add your ribs and any juices into the pot, cover and let it steam for 10 minutes. Set a timer. This will infuse your ribs with the stock and red wine.

4. Preheat oven 375 F, lightly grease a baking sheet. Once your time goes off. Turn off the heat for your stove, and using tongs, carefully transfer each rib to your baking sheet. Bake in middle rack of your hot oven for 20 minutes. Set timer.

5. Once timer goes off, remove the ribs and serve immediately. Serve with your favorite salad.

Classic Hamburger Helper

COOK TIME
25 MIN
PREP TIME
10 MIN
SERVINGS
4 SERVINGS

INGREDIENTS

- 1 pound of minced beef
- 1 tablespoon dark soy sauce
- 1 large onion, diced
- 2 cups of sliced white mushrooms
- 1 medium sized carrot, chopped
- 2 medium sized tomatoes, chopped
- ½ cup frozen corn
- 2 cloves minced garlic
- 3 cups beef broth
- 2 cups tomato sauce
- 1 cup tomato paste
- 3 cups dried macaroni
- ½ tablespoon dried parsley flakes
- ½ tablespoon oregano
- 1 tablespoon sriracha
- 1 tablespoon sesame oil
- 2 cups grated sharp yellow cheddar
- 1 green scallion chopped (fresh garnish)
- 1 small tomato diced (fresh garnish)
- Salt and Pepper to taste

PREPARATION

1. In a large mixing bowl season your beef with soy sauce, parsley flakes, oregano, sriracha and a pinch of black pepper. Set aside. In a medium skillet, sauté the onions and garlic with the sesame oil until tender, about 2 to 3 minutes. Stir in the diced tomatoes and sauté for another minute.

2. Add in your marinated beef and sauté until brown. Combine the rest of your ingredients: mushrooms, corn, beef broth, tomato sauce, and tomato paste. Mix well. When the sauce is bubbling, stir in your dry pasta. Make sure the pasta is fully submerged in the sauce.

3. Cover the skillet with a lid and simmer on Medium Low until the pasta softens and the sauce has thicken slightly.

Gently stir in the cheddar and chopped green scallions. Taste, and adjust the seasoning to your liking. Serve in individual bowls with a sprinkle of fresh, diced, tomatoes and freshly cracked black pepper.

Notes

Easy Beef Stroganoff

COOK TIME
25 MIN
PREP TIME
10 MIN
SERVINGS
6 SERVINGS

INGREDIENTS

- 2 pounds of beef round steak cut into one inch pieces
- 1 large onion, diced
- 2 cups of sliced white mushrooms
- 1 cup of tomato sauce
- ½ tablespoon dried parsley flakes
- 1 tablespoon minced fresh garlic
- 1 cup beef broth
- 1 teaspoon butter
- 1 tablespoon olive oil
- Salt and Pepper to taste
- 1/3 cup of sour cream for serving
- Fresh parsley leaves for garnish

PREPARATION

1. In a medium mixing bowl, season your beef with two small pitches of salt and black pepper. Set aside.

2. In a smaller mixing bowl, whisk together the following ingredients:
   - 1 cup of tomato sauce
   - ½ tablespoon dried parsley flakes
   - 1 tablespoon minced fresh garlic
   - 1 cup beef broth

3. In a medium non-stick skillet, add in the butter and olive oil. Once the butter has melted and the olive oil is hot, quickly brown your beef for 2 minutes.

4. Add in the diced onion and white mushrooms and sauté for another 2 minutes.

5. Stir in the whisked ingredients and cover with a lid. Let the mixture simmer on Medium Low heat for 15 minutes.

6. When the mixture has reduced and thickened slightly, give it a gentle stir and taste. Season with salt and paper. Serve over pasta, or egg noodles, with a dollop of sour cream. Garnish with fresh parsley leaves.

Mushroom Onion Gravy Pork Chops

COOK TIME
25 MIN
PREP TIME
5 MIN
SERVINGS
4-6 SERVINGS

INGREDIENTS

- 4 bone-in thick pork chops
- 2 tablespoons olive oil
- 1 ½ cups water
- 1 can condensed cream of mushroom soup
- 1 cup of mushrooms, sliced
- Lemon pepper

PREPARATION

1. Rinse and pat the pork chops dry. Season the meat liberally with Lemon Pepper (or with your favorite seasoning).
2. Over Medium High heat, add olive oil to a non-stick skillet and brown the pork chops on both sides. When browned set the pork chops aside. In the same skillet, pour in water to deglaze the pot. Give the pan a quick stir and then mix in the cream of mushroom soup and onions. When the mixture comes to a boil, lower the heat to Medium Low, and add the pork chops back into the skillet.
3. Cover the pan and let it simmer on for about 20 minutes or until the pork chops are fully cooked. Stir occasionally. Serve each pork chop over a bed of rice or pasta and pour the mushroom gravy over the pork chops.

SEAFOOD LOVERS

Popcorn Shrimp

COOK TIME
10 MIN
PREP TIME
10 MIN
SERVINGS
4 SERVINGS

INGREDIENTS

- 2-3 pounds medium size shrimp, thawed and peeled
- 1 tablespoon salt
- 2 tablespoon pepper
- 2 tablespoon sesame oil
- 2 cup panko crumbs (Panko is a Japanese style breadcrumbs)
- 1 cup breadcrumbs
- ½ cup flour
- 3 eggs

PREPARATION

1. Preheat the oven to 350 F.

2. In a large mixing bowl, beat 3 eggs with sesame oil, salt, and pepper. Add in the shrimp and coat it evenly with the egg mixture. Set aside.

3. In another large mixing bowl toss together the panko, breadcrumbs and flour. Add in a pinch of salt and pepper.

4. Use a wire mesh strainer to remove the excess egg mixture from the shrimp. Toss the shrimp into the breadcrumb mix and coat the shrimp evenly.

5. On a baking sheet lined with parchment paper, lay the shrimp flat, with enough space between each shrimp. Pop the baking sheet into the preheated oven and bake for 10 minutes, or until golden brown, making sure to flip the shrimp half way for even cooking.

6. Serve with fresh celery sticks, lemon wedges, and your favorite dipping sauce.

Summer Salmon and Dill

COOK TIME
15 MIN
PREP TIME
10 MIN
SERVINGS
2 SERVINGS

INGREDIENTS

- 2 fresh salmon filets
- 2 tablespoons soy sauce
- 2 tablespoons sea salt
- 2 tablespoon white pepper
- 4 tablespoons dried dill
- 2 springs of fresh dill
- 2 tablespoon sesame oil
- 4 slices of fresh lemon

PREPARATION

1. Preheat oven to 375 F. In small mixing bowl whisk together, soy sauce, sea salt, white pepper, dill flakes, and sesame oil. Add the salmon filets into the mixture and marinate for at least 5 minutes.

2. Place the salmon filets onto a large baking sheet lined with parchment paper. Lay a sprig of fresh dill on each filet and then line the tops of the fish with slices of fresh lemon. Bake uncovered for 15 minutes, or until the fish is flaky.

3. Serve the salmon over a bread of crisp salad greens and freshly cracked pepper.

Crispy Fish Sticks

COOK TIME
15-20 MIN
PREP TIME
15 MIN
SERVINGS
4 SERVINGS

INGREDIENTS

- 2 pounds fresh halibut, or cod, cut into sticks
- 1 tablespoon salt
- 2 tablespoon white pepper
- 2 tablespoon dried parsley flakes
- 2 tablespoon soy sauce
- 1 tablespoon sesame oil
- 2 cups panko mixed with 1 cup seasoned breadcrumbs
- ½ cup flour
- 2 eggs

PREPARATION

1. Preheat the oven to 400 F.

2. In large mixing bowl gently coat the fish sticks with sesame oil, soy sauce, salt, white pepper and dried parsley flakes. Let the fish marinate in the mixture for 5 minutes.

3. In a separate bowl, beat the eggs until foamy. Remove the fish from the marinade, and dip each fish stick into the egg before coating it with the breadcrumb mix. Repeat with the remaining pieces of fish.

4. Line a baking sheet with parchment paper and lay the fish sticks flat, leaving enough room between each one for even cooking. Bake until the coating is golden brown and the fish flakes easily with a fork – about 15 minutes. For even browning, flip the fish halfway through the cooking time.

5. Serve with a chili tartar sauce and fresh cucumber slices.

VEGETABLE LOVERS

Mama's Fried Brussels Sprouts

COOK TIME
25-30 MIN
PREP TIME
10 MIN
SERVINGS
4 SERVINGS

INGREDIENTS

- 1 pound of Brussels sprouts, trimmed and yellowed leaves removed
- ½ cup of parmesan powder
- 2 tablespoon olive oil
- 1 tablespoon sesame oil
- 1 tablespoon salt
- 1 tablespoon white pepper

PREPARATION

1. Preheat oven to 400 F. In large mixing bowl, toss Brussels sprouts with parmesan powder, olive oil, sesame oil, salt, and pepper. Lightly grease a baking sheet and lay your Brussel sprouts onto it, and bake for 30 minutes. Make sure to give the pan a shake every 5 minutes for even cooking. Set timer. Once timer goes off your Brussel sprouts are ready.

Roasted Garlic Fried Broccoli

COOK TIME
25 MIN
PREP TIME
10 MIN
SERVINGS
4 SERVINGS

INGREDIENTS

- 1-2 heads of broccoli, washed and cut into bite sized chunks
- 1 tablespoon salt
- 2 tablespoon pepper
- 3 tablespoon garlic powder
- 2 tablespoon onion flakes
- 2 tablespoon sesame oil

PREPARATION

1. In large mixing bowl, toss the broccoli chunks with the above ingredients. Make sure each broccoli chunk is well coated. Preheat oven to 375 F then distribute the broccoli chunks evenly in a baking sheet and bake for 25 minutes. Set timer. Once timer goes off, serve on platter with ranch dipping sauce or a blue cheese sauce.

Parmesan Fried Cauliflower

COOK TIME
15 MIN
PREP TIME
5 MIN
SERVINGS
4 SERVINGS

INGREDIENTS

- 1 head cauliflower, rinsed and chopped in bite sized chunks
- ¼ cup parmesan powder
- 2 tablespoon dried parsley flakes
- 1 tablespoon salt
- 2 tablespoon white pepper
- 1 tablespoon sesame oil

PREPARATION

1. Preheat the oven to 450 F. In a large mixing bowl toss the cauliflower with parmesan powder, parsley flakes, salt, white pepper, and sesame oil. Pour the coated cauliflower onto a greased baking sheet and bake for 15 minutes, making sure to give the cauliflower a stir every 5 minutes for even cooking and to avoid burning.

2. When the cauliflower is golden brown and tender, take it out of the oven and serve as a snack or toss it into a salad to add texture and more flavor.

Toasted Sesame Seed Kale Chips

COOK TIME
10-15 MIN
PREP TIME
10 MIN
SERVINGS
2 SERVINGS

INGREDIENTS

- 1 bunch of kale
- 1½ tablespoon sea salt
- 1 tablespoon olive oil
- 2 tablespoon sesame oil
- ½ table spoon red chili flakes
- Toasted sesame seeds for garnish

PREPARATION

1. Preheat the oven to 350 F. Thoroughly wash the kale and pat dry with a clean towel or paper towels. Separate the kale leaves from its thick stalk and roughly chop the leaves.

2. In large mixing bowl toss the kale with the sea salt, olive oil, sesame oil and chili flakes. Lay the kale leaves in a single layer on a greased baking sheet. Bake for the kale leaves until crisp and the edges are slightly brown, about 10-15 minutes.

3. Serve the kale chips with your favorite soup and sandwich or as a healthy and tasty alternative to potato chips.

Garlicky Fried Bok Choy

COOK TIME
10 MIN
PREP TIME
10 MIN
SERVINGS
4 SERVINGS

INGREDIENTS

- ½ pound of baby bok choy, washed and pat dry
- 2 tablespoon sea salt
- 2 tablespoon white pepper
- 3 tablespoon garlic powder
- 3 tablespoon sesame oil

PREPARATION

1. Preheat the oven to 450 F. In large mixing bowl, toss the baby bok choy with sea salt, white pepper, garlic powder, and sesame oil. Make sure the leaves are well coated with the seasoning and oil.
2. Lay the baby bok choy in a single layer on a greased baking sheet and bake for 10 minutes or until the leaves are slightly crispy and the body is a warm caramel color. Serve as a side to your favorite fried rice or homemade stew.

Chili Oil Green Beans

COOK TIME
5 MIN
PREP TIME
5 MIN
SERVINGS
2 SERVINGS

INGREDIENTS

- 1 pound of long green beans with the ends trimmed
- 1 tablespoon sea salt
- 2 tablespoon Sriracha sauce
- 3 tablespoon chili oil
- 1 tablespoon sesame oil

PREPARATION

1. In a large mixing bowl toss the green beans with sea salt, Sriracha sauce, chili oil, and sesame oil. Heat a medium, non-stick, skillet on High heat. Add the green beans and stir-fry for 3-5 minutes until the green beans turn dark green and the sauce has caramelized.
2. Serve over jasmine rice or as a side to your favorite fried rice

Parsley Baked Potatoes

COOK TIME
35-40 MIN
PREP TIME
10 MIN
SERVINGS
2 SERVINGS

INGREDIENTS

- 2 medium sized potatoes for baking (you can substitute for yams for a healthy alternative)
- 2 tablespoons sesame oil
- 1 tablespoon salt
- 2 tablespoon garlic powder
- 2 tablespoon dried parsley flakes

PREPARATION

1. Preheat the oven to 425 F. Thoroughly wash potatoes under running water and pat dry. With a fork, prick the potatoes to help allow steam to escape during the cooking process. Combine the seasonings to make a spice mix. Generously rub the potatoes with sesame oil and the spice mix.
2. Place the potatoes onto a baking sheet and bake for 35-40 minutes, or until the skin is crispy and a fork pierces through easily.
3. Serve with sour cream and your favorite toppings to make it into a simple meal on its own, or as a side to your dish.

DESSERT

It does not just end with dinner.

There's always room for dessert! I've curated some of my favorite dessert recipes that would go great with your home cooked meals.

Happy Eating,

Julia Moore

Mini Open-Face Blackberry Pie

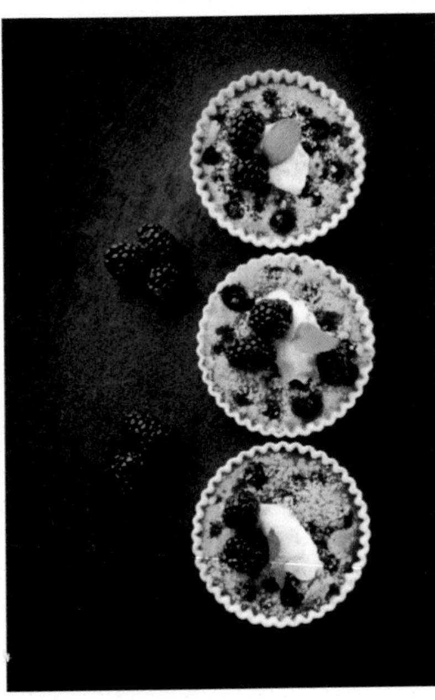

INGREDIENTS

- 5 cups fresh blackberries
- ½ cup blackberry jam
- ½ cup brown sugar
- 1 teaspoon cinnamon
- 1 teaspoon lemon juice
- 1 teaspoon lemon zest
- 1 cup water
- 1 cup crushed graham cracker crumbs
- 1 package of ready-made puff pastry
- ½ cup all-purpose flour
- ½ tablespoon cornstarch mixed with 1 tablespoon water
- ½ cup melted butter for brushing
- Fresh whipped cream and more blackberries for garnish

PREPARATION

1. Dust countertop with the flour and roll out the ready-made puff pastry, about half inch thick. Butter 4 ramekins. Cut the puff pastry into squares and mould it into your 4 ramekins and use a sharp knife to trim excess dough off. Brush the puff pastry with melted butter and set aside. Preheat your oven to 350 F. Bake in middle rack 10 minutes, or until golden brown.

2. Once it's done take it out of the oven and set aside.

3. In a small non-stick sauce pot add in the water, brown sugar, lemon juice, lemon zest, blackberries and blackberry jam. Cook on medium-high for 15-20 minutes reducing the liquid, stir constantly. Taste it for sweetness. Then slowly stir in the cornstarch mixture, this will thicken your blackberry filling. Then evenly distribute the blackberry filling into your 4 ramekins and sprinkle a layer of graham cracker crumbs on top, pop it back into the oven and bake for another 10 minutes, until you get a nice crisp on top. Serve with fresh whipped cream and more blackberries.

Mango Tapioca Pudding

PLEASE NOTE: THE RECIPE REQUIRES A PRESSURE COOKER POT.

INGREDIENTS

- ½ cup white pearl tapioca (small kind)
- 2 cups coconut milk
- ½ cup water
- ½ cup sugar
- ½ teaspoon vanilla extract
- 1 cup frozen mangoes blended in a blender with ¼ cup sugar until smooth.
- Fresh mango diced into cubes to serve
- ½ tablespoon cornstarch mixed with 1 tablespoon water.

PREPARATION

1. Add the tapioca, coconut milk, water, sugar, and vanilla extract into your pressure cooking pot. Stir to combine, then lock lid and cook on High for 7 minutes. Set timer. Once timer goes off release pressure naturally, and stir in the cornstarch mixture.

2. Bring to a boil then stir in your mango puree for about 1 minute. Turn off pressure cooker and spoon the mango tapioca into individual dessert glasses. Let it chill in the fridge for an hour. Serve with fresh mangos and a drizzle of honey.

Notes

After Dinner Chocolate Mousse

INGREDIENTS

- ½ cup milk, at room temperature
- 1 cup olive oil (you don't necessary need to use it all, but it really helps keep the chocolate smooth)
- 1 cup Dark Chocolate, chopped up
- 1 cup Semi-Sweet Chocolate, chopped up
- 2 cups plus 2 tablespoon heavy Cream whipped to stiff peaks, divided
  1 cup fresh raspberries

PREPARATION

1. Whip your heavy cream first, once it's whipped keep cool in fridge.

2. In a small double-boiler add in about half a cup of the olive oil first and warm it up on medium-high heat. Add the dark chocolate and begin mixing with a silicone whisk. Once the dark chocolate is almost melted, add in the Semi-Sweet Chocolate and add in a bit more olive oil. Whisk until smooth, then slowly add in your milk and continue whisking until smooth. You do not need to add more olive oil if the chocolate is completely melted and smooth – it should resemble a glossy surface (roughly 10 minutes for everything to melt and smoothen out).

3. Let the melted chocolate cool to room temperate before adding it in your whipped cream. Begin folding half of your melted chocolate into it with a silicone spatula. Do not stir. Keep folding until you have mixed in all your cream and chocolate (2 minutes).

4. To serve, spoon the chocolate mousse into wine glasses or dessert bowls, add the fresh raspberries and a dusting of powdered sugar and mint leaves for garnish. You can serve this with just about any type of fresh fruits and nuts.

THANK YOU

We sincerely hope you enjoyed cooking with us!

Julia Moore

80147600R00058

Made in the USA
San Bernardino, CA
23 June 2018